Pennsylvania Cavalry 4th Regt., William Emile Doster

A Brief History of the Fourth Pennsylvania Veteran Cavalry

embracing organization, reunions, dedication of monument at Gettysburg and

address of General W. E. Doster, Venango County Battalion, reminiscences, etc

Pennsylvania Cavalry 4th Regt., William Emile Doster

A Brief History of the Fourth Pennsylvania Veteran Cavalry
embracing organization, reunions, dedication of monument at Gettysburg and address of
General W. E. Doster, Venango County Battalion, reminiscences, etc

ISBN/EAN: 9783337734275

Printed in Europe, USA, Canada, Australia, Japan

Cover: Foto ©Andreas Hilbeck / pixelio.de

More available books at **www.hansebooks.com**

A

BRIEF HISTORY

OF THE

FOURTH

Pennsylvania Veteran Cavalry,

EMBRACING

ORGANIZATION, REUNIONS,
DEDICATION OF MONUMENT AT GETTYSBURG AND
ADDRESS OF GENERAL W. E. DOSTER,
VENANGO COUNTY BATTALION,
REMINISCENCES, ETC.

PUBLISHED AT PITTSBURGH, PA.

EWENS & EBERLE, BOOK AND JOB PRINTERS, COR. FOURTH AVENUE AND WOOD STREET.

1891.

549
3249

Pennsylvania cavalry. *4th regt.*, 1861–1865.

A brief history of the Fourth Pennsylvania Veteran cavalry, embracing organization, reunions, dedication of monument at Gettysburg and address of General W. E. Doster, Venango County battalion, reminiscences, etc. Pittsburgh, Pa., Ewens & Eberle, printers, 1891.

113 p. 23½ᶜᵐ.

✳ FOURTH ✳

PENNSYLVANIA

✳ CAVALRY ✳

"Fling out our Country's banner wide,
    Our emblematic, starry gem ;
Our Union never shall divide,
    While floats the silken diadem.
Year after year the brilliant stars
    Shall indicate the strength of all ;
Let all beware of civil wars,
    Her patriot's wound, and traitor's fall."   M.

INTRODUCTION.

COMRADES:—A beginning has been made towards the accomplishment of the end sought, namely, a complete history of the regiment. This can only be done through your hearty co-operation—and not otherwise. The history of this grand organization is largely locked up in your memories, and we want the facts which you can furnish to make this enterprise a success. By publishing each year the proceedings of our reunions and making them replete with fact and incident of the part borne by you, and having access to all the records on file, we shall be able, in time, to commemorate in history the valor and patriotism of the men who gave themselves, unreservedly, to the cause of their country in its hour of peril, and perpetuated, one and indivisible, the Union of the States in a grand and glorious compact, which insures to all the most perfect freedom of conscience and action as good citizens of the grandest republic of the world. Trusting that this venture will be received in the spirit which has actuated the Committee in its preparation, we send it forth as the first number of a history which will be continued as long as there are members of the Fourth Pennsylvania Veteran Cavalry left to compile and read it, and thus leave to our children something to inspire true loyalty in their hearts and the satisfaction of having the deeds of loved ones on record.

PUBLISHING COMMITTEE.

PROPOSED HISTORY OF FOURTH REGIMENT
PENNSYLVANIA CAVALRY.

The object of publishing such a work is to place on permanent record marches, battles and experiences of the officers and men who composed this regiment.

DEAR COMRADE :—

We have been employing some of our time in searching for matters and documents relating to the Fourth Regiment. We want a complete record of its progress from time of its organization to its muster out.

Will you answer the following questions? sending same to J. B. MAITLAND, Historian, Oil City, Pa.:

When and where did you enlist?

When and where mustered out?

Were you drafted or a substitute?

Were you in any battles or skirmishes; when and where?

Note any acts of bravery, wounds received, and where?

Were you in any rebel prison?

Where were you captured?

Do you know of any comrades dying in prison? Name place and date.

When and where were you paroled?

Were you promoted while in the army?

If you were promoted, to what position?

Were you on detailed duty? If so, when and where?

What is your present address?

We trust you will reply *promptly* and *fully*, so we can make a complete history. Now, don't lay this aside; it is to your interest to attend to this at once.

Yours truly,

PUBLISHING COMMITTEE.

HISTORY

OF THE

FOURTH PENNSYLVANIA CAVALRY.

·

ORGANIZATION.

The Fourth Cavalry was recruited in compliance with authority granted by Governor Curtin, dated September 4th, 1861. Company A was recruited in Northampton County; B, E and G in Allegheny County; C and D in Westmoreland and Indiana Counties; H, I, K and L in Venango County; F in Lebanon County, and M in Luzerne County. The companies rendezvoused at Camp Curtin; were transferred from there to Camp Campbell, on Meridian Hill, Washington, D. C., where the men were mustered into the United States service, and were organized in three battalions of four companies each. The State colors were presented by Governor Curtin, in person, on the 20th of September, 1861, and were received on behalf of the Regiment by the Commading Officer, David Campbell.

Original enlistment (1861)...... 1,006
Re-enlisted and recruited................ ... 924

      Total enrollment............ 1,930

Mustered in from August 15th to October 30th, 1861.
Mustered out July 1st, 1865.

· ·

BATTLES

Participated in by the Fourth Pennsylvania Veteran Cavalry,
as shown by the records of the War Department : -

MECHANICSVILLE.
GAINES' MILL.
GLENDALE.
MALVERN HILL.
ANTIETAM.
HEDGESVILLE.
UNION.
UPPERVILLE, Nov. 3, 1862.
MANASSAS GAP.
MARKHAM STATION.
LITTLE WASHINGTON.
GAINES' CROSS ROADS.
WATERLOO.
FREDERICKSBURG.
KELLY'S FORD.
RAPIDAN STATION.
CHANCELLORSVILLE.
STEVENSBURG.
MIDDLEBURG.
UPPERVILLE, June 21, 1863.
GETTYSBURG.
GREEN OAK.
SHEPHERDSTOWN.
NEWBY'S CROSS ROADS.
MUDDY RUN.
CULPEPPER.
SULPHUR SPRINGS.
BRISTOE STATION.
KILPATRICK'S RAID.
WILDERNESS.
SPOTTSYLVANIA.

NORTH ANNA.
GROUND SQUIRREL CHURCH.
GLEN ALLEN STATION.
YELLOW TAVERN.
BROOK CHURCH.
HAWES' SHOP.
OLD CHURCH.
COLD HARBOR.
TREVILIAN STATION.
MACON'S HILL.
ST. MARY'S CHURCH.
PETERSBURG.
WARWICK SWAMP.
STRAWBERRY PLAIN.
LEE'S MILL.
DEEP BOTTOM.
REAM'S STATION.
POPLAR SPRING CHURCH.
FALL'S CHURCH.
WYATT'S FARM.
BOYDTON ROAD.
STONY CREEK STATION.
BELLEFIELD.
HATCHER'S RUN.
DINWIDDIE COURT HOUSE.
PAYNE'S CROSS ROADS.
AMELIA SPRINGS.
SAILOR'S CREEK.
FARMVILLE.
APPOMATTOX.

and 16 additional engagements, making a total of 77 battles
and skirmishes, in which the Regiment lost in killed and
wounded :

CASUALTIES.

Killed and died of wounds...	101
Died of disease..........	230
Died of other causes..........	25
Wounded..........	224
Captured or missing..........	271
Total casualties..........	851

About 100 additional members were killed and wounded, of which no record is given.

FIRST REUNION.

Pursuant to a call made August 10th, 1875, members of the Fourth Pennsylvania Cavalry, residing in Allegheny County, convened and organized a society for the purpose of effecting a permanent organization of all the surviving members of the regiment.

The following officers were elected to serve until the first reunion would take place, and adopt a Constitution and By-Laws :

PRESIDENT,	- -	COL. A. P. DUNCAN,
VICE PRESIDENT,	-	MAJ. D. C. PHILLIPS,
REC. SECRETARY,	-	C. P. SEIP, M. D.,
COR. SECRETARY,	-	J. J. GREEN, M. D.,
TREASURER,	- -	ALEX. MATCHETT, ESQ.

On September 17th, 1875, nearly two hundred members of the Regiment convened in Pittsburgh at the first reunion. The meeting was called to order by Col. A. P. Duncan ; the Constitution and By-Laws were then adopted, and the following officers were elected to serve during the ensuing year :

PRESIDENT,	- -	MAJ. W. N. BIDDLE,
VICE PRESIDENT,	-	MAJ. J. C. PAUL,
REC. SECRETARY,	-	ISAAC MILLER, ESQ.,
COR. SECRETARY,	-	J. J. GREEN, M. D.,
TREASURER,	- -	W. H. COLLINGWOOD.

EXECUTIVE COMMITTEE:

COL. A. P. DUNCAN,   MAJ. D. C. PHILLIPS,
CAPT. HUGHES.

HISTORIAN,   -   -   C. P. SEIP, M. D.

Orations were then delivered by Col. J. S. Haymaker and others, in Turner Hall, from which the Regiment adjourned to the St. Charles Hotel, where a banquet was participated in by all concerned, after which the society adjourned to meet at the call of the Executive Committee.

CONSTITUTION.

ARTICLE I.

TITLE.

The name and title of this association shall be the SOCIETY OF THE FOURTH PENNSYLVANIA CAVALRY.

ARTICLE II.

OBJECTS.

The objects of this society shall be to perpetuate the memory of the Fourth Regiment Pennsylvania Volunteer Cavalry; it fortunes and achievements. To promote and maintain the kindly and cordial feelings which should exist between men who have faced dangers and hardships in the same cause, and to collect and preserve proper memorials of our fallen comrades.

ARTICLE III.

MEMBERS AND HONORARY MEMBERS.

Any officer or soldier who at any time served honorably in the Fourth Pennsylvania Cavalry is entitled to membership.

Officers and soldiers who became distinguished in other regiments or commands, and distinguished citizens, may be elected to honorary membership.

ARTICLE IV.

ORGANIZATION.

This society shall be organized by the annual election of a President, a Vice-President, a Corresponding Secretary, a Recording Secretary, and a Treasurer.

ARTICLE V.

MEETINGS.

The society shall meet once a year. The time and place of next meeting to be selected by ballot at each meeting.

All members unable to attend personally, at any meeting, are expected to notify the Corresponding Secretary, and to impart such information in regard to themselves as they may think proper, and as may be of interest to their brethren of the society.

BY-LAWS.

I.   All meetings of this society shall be opened by prayer.

II.   Every officer and soldier desiring to become a member of this Association, shall pay to the Treasurer thereof an initiation fee of the sum of one dollar, and the sum of two dollars as yearly dues thereafter, by which he shall be presumed as subscribing his assent to the Constitution and By-Laws, and shall thereupon be entitled to a copy free of charge. Such dues to be payable at, or before each annual reunion.

III.   Any member who shall be in arrears for dues for a period of two years, shall be dropped from the rolls.

IV.   All moneys paid out by the Treasurer shall be on the written order of the Recording Secretary, endorsed by the President; and at each annual meeting the Treasurer shall make a full report of his receipts and expenditures.

V.   At each annual meeting the President shall appoint a committee of three members, not officers of the society, to audit all claims against, and accounts of the society.

VI.   When the place of the next annual meeting is fixed, the President shall appoint an Executive Committee of three (3) members, residing at or accessible to the place of meeting, whose duty it shall be to make all needful preparations and arrangements for such meeting.

VII.   No member shall speak more than once on any matter of business, and no longer than five minutes without consent of the society first obtained.

VIII.   At each annual meeting there shall be selected, in such manner as the society shall determine, a person to deliver an address at the next annual meeting.

IX.   No petitions for the relief of members shall be circulated at the reunions. Such cases shall be reported to the society, and relief ordered out of any funds not otherwise appropriated.

X.   At any annual reunion the Constitution or By-Laws may be amended by a vote of two-thirds the members present.

Our first General Order :

GENERAL ORDER No. 1.

MAJOR J. B. MAITLAND, ESQ.:

SIR:—You will please remit to W. H. Collingwood, Treasurer, No. 715 Liberty Street, Pittsburgh, Pa., the amount of enclosed bill, at your earliest convenience, as it is not only desirable, but necessary, that the Regimental Organization be thus fortified and equipped as soon as practicable, in that it may immediately advance in good order to prepare for the forthcoming annual reunion. Where it may be possible to do so, remit by Post Office Order, Registered Letter. or by a Draft on a Pittsburgh Bank; and, on receipt of the amount of enclosed bill from all those who are not already members of the Association, their names will be immediately enrolled as such.

You will please forward to C. P. Seip, M. D., Historian, No. 636 Penn Avenue, Pittsburgh, Pa., a succinct statement of all historical events and incidents con-

nected with the history of the Regiment, of which you may have some memoranda. or personal recollection—the object of which is to be able to compile, from the mass of information thus contributed by individual members, an elaborate. authentic, and complete History of the Regiment, ranging from its organization to its disbandment. All diaries, documents, or scraps of history in whatever shape. will again be returned to their owners, if by them desired.

You will please communicate to J. J. Green, M. D., Corresponding Secretary. No. 2530 Penn Avenue, Pittsburgh, Pa., your own address in full, and in plain and legible handwriting, together with the addresses of all the members of the Regiment of which you may be cognizant, or which you may now, or hereafter obtain: and, when you, at any time, shall have changed your place of abode, you are requested to thereupon notify the Corresponding Secretary of the fact, and to again communicate to him your address in full as before.

By order of Executive Committee,

ISAAC MILLER, *Rec. Secretary.*

MAJ. W. N. BIDDLE, *President.*

PITTSBURGH, PA., September 25th, 1876.

SIR:—The Annual Reunion of the Fourth Pennsylvania Veteran Cavalry, will be held at Franklin, Venango County, Pa., on October 12th, 1876. The fare from Pittsburgh and intermediate points, as far as West Penn Junction to Franklin and return, will be only Four Dollars for the round trip. Train leaves Union Depot, Pittsburgh, at 8:25, P. M., on October 11th, and returning arrives at Pittsburgh at 6 o'clock, A. M., on Friday, October 13th, 1876.

Please notify Corresponding Secretary by return mail, if you will be present. Present this Card when you apply for ticket at R. R. Office.

By order of Executive Committee.

Address, DR. J. J. GREEN, *Cor. Secretary,*

No. 2530 Penn Avenue, PITTSBURGH, PA.

PITTSBURGH, PA., September 28th, 1876

DEAR SIR:—The second Annual Reunion of the Fourth Pennsylvania Vet. Cavalry, will be held in Franklin, Venango County, Pa., Thursday, October 12, 1876. As a large delegation is expected from Pittsburgh, we earnestly request all the members of the Regiment in and about the Oil Regions to be in attendance.

By order of Executive Committee,

Address, J. J. GREEN, M. D., *Cor. Secretary,*

No. 2530 Penn Avenue, PITTSBURGH, PA.

SECOND REUNION.

The second reunion was held at Franklin, Pa., October 12th, 1876. The town was finely decorated for the occasion, and the display of bunting was large. Flags were waving from all the principal stores on Liberty Street, while a grand Centennial flag was stretched across the street near the Court House. In the profuse display of decorations on any patriotic occasion, Franklin leads all the towns in this section.

At an early hour the guests arrived and gathered in the rooms of the Sportsmen's Club. A business meeting was held here and the following officers elected for the coming year: President, Captain John P. Barr; Vice President, Captain W. M. Shortts; Corresponding Secretary, Lieutenant L. D. Davis; Recording Secretary, Captain J. R. Grant; Treasurer, Lieutenant C. S. Mark. Post A. B. McCalmont, No. 160, G. A. R., from Oil City, was present and joined with the veterans in their reunion.

At the conclusion of the business meeting, the veterans, about eighty in number, and Post A. B. McCalmont, escorted by the Venango Greys and Greys' Band, proceeded to the Soldiers' Monument. The veterans presented a fine appearance with their soldierly bearing, and the Venango Greys, under the command of Captain Wiley, made a favorable impression. At the monument arms were presented, heads uncovered and a few moments passed in honor of the dead, when the procession returned to the Association rooms.

At 5 o'clock a grand banquet was given at the Exchange Hotel, at which many of the prominent citizens of Franklin were present. When each one had satisfied himself with the excellent spread an adjournment was made to the Association rooms. A business meeting was held, at which the following resolutions were passed:

Resolved, That the thanks of this association are hereby tendered to J. Morton Hall, General Ticket Agent, and the officials of the Allegheny Valley Railroad, for the favors shown the society at this reunion.

Resolved, That we heartily thank the Venango Greys, the Venango Grey's Band and Post General A. B. McCalmont No. 160, G. A. R., of Oil City, for their courtesy and attention to this Association.

Resolved, That we return our thanks to the Sportsmen's Club of Franklin, for their kindness in allowing this Association the use of their rooms.

Resolved, That these resolutions be published in the Oil City Derrick and Franklin papers.

The following persons were also made honorary members of the Association: Captain James B. Clew, Pittsburgh; John H. Covode, West Chester; William Collingwood, Pittsburgh; E. M. Biddle, Pittsburgh; Mrs. Jane Welton, Franklin; Marshall Kerr, Kerrtown; Capt. John A. Wiley, Franklin; J. Morton Hall, Pittsburgh.

The Pittsburgh delegation consisted of Maj. W. N. Biddle, John T. Ewens, William H. Collingwood, Major J. C. Paul, Adjt. J. E. B. Dalzell, Capt. W. K. Gillespie and Isaac Miller.

At the conclusion of business the members marched to the Court House, escorted by the Venango Greys and Band. While the veterans were passing through Liberty Street cannon were fired and loud cheers given. A good audience gathered at the Court House to listen to the address of Capt. C. E. Taylor. He spoke as a soldier to soldiers; referring to the fitness of such reunions, and the memories they stirred in a soldier's heart. We give below the synopsis of his remarks:

ADDRESS OF CAPT. C. E. TAYLOR.

COMRADES OF THE FOURTH PENN'A CAVALRY:—

While I hardly know how to find words to express my gratitude to you for the honor you have done me in asking me to address you. I can, at the same time, truthfully say, I do not know when you could have called upon me that I could not more nearly have done justice to you and myself. My mind has been full of so many matters for the past month or two, that it seemed to me when you first asked me to address you, that I must peremptorily refuse. But my love for the old regiment got the better of my judgment, and I reluctantly consented to try and say something about our old associations; for of all the associations of my life, none are dearer to me to-day than those formed during my connection

with the noble old Fourth. Looking away back so many years, I can hardly remember of a single man in that whole command, that I could not have taken by the hand and called him my friend and brother—all bound together by the most sacred ties—ties woven by mutual hardships, dangers and privations, into the most tender and affectionate relations possible for man to form. Yes, the associations formed by us at a time when all the restraints of home were taken off, though rude and unpolished in many respects, were associations of the heart—associations which only death can obliterate, and even after death, in that bright world beyond the stars, I firmly believe that the associations formed at Gaines' Mill, Antietam, Gettysburg and other fields where death, in its most horrid form became your comrade, will be renewed again, and that when renewed they will continue throughout the countless cycles of eternity. You may think this an extravagant thought ; but it is a most beautiful one to contemplate, and I believe that our anticipation of such a happy reunion, will not only be fully realized in that far off and unknown land, but will make us purer and better here. There are no friends like those who have faced death together, and no associations like those formed in the " imminent deadly breach." * *

The lights and shadows, joys and sorrows, trials and disappointments of more than fifteen years have glided past, since our first Colonel, David Campbell, received authority from the Governor of the State to recruit and organize the regiment, afterwards known as the Fourth Pennsylvania Cavalry. This was the formation of our union. To create that union its very basis was necessarily disunion, and every department, every relation of life was ruthlessly invaded. Long years of union in the varied pursuits of life were dissolved; business ruined, and fortunes wrecked ; political ties and lifelong friendships like gossamer threads were snapped asunder; even the sacred precincts of the altar were no protection, and consequently the church dissolved the union of nearly half her members. The domestic circle was also invaded, and in the severing of that union of the family at home was felt the sharpest, keenest pang—the very agony of despair. The

father bade his boy a long good-by ; sister from her brother parted, maiden from her lover, the wife gave up her husband, and with the severing of these ties, years of bright hopes and happy anticipations were blasted into life-long misery and sorrow. The gray haired mother sank upon her knees, as from her very soul in agony was wrung the prayer :—" If it be possible let this cup pass from me ; if not, Oh. God of battles, protect Thou my pride, my darling boy." Truly, our Union was born in sorrow, baptized in tears, cemented with blood ; and from the very depths of human suffering and woe, it gathered strength for its many fearful struggles and sacrifices. Under such circumstances was the union of our regiment formed. Its object I will not dwell upon. Suffice it to say, it was not that we might learn the art of war, and surely it was not a mercenary object. Thirteen dollars a month for being made a target was not a luxury sought by any. Oh, no; it was an object, grand, noble and worthy of our loftiest aspirations and most costly sacrifices. It dealt with the vital interests of the whole human race, for all time to come, and stamped its impress upon the records of eternity.

But this union has left its impress upon us all. Yet, who among us, if he could, would exchange for a King's ransom, or for aught that wealth could purchase, the experience and knowledge, that brings to each, the heartfelt satisfaction of knowing the fact, that he was one who in some measure helped to bring about the grand result. Nay, I tell you there was more of duty well performed, more of sacrifice, more of life, more of death, and more of grand results crowded into that four years of our union, than seldom falls to the lot of man, in thrice the three score years and ten. During these fifteen years that have elapsed since the union of our regiment was formed, what a wonderful transformation has been wrought ! What changes have come over our country, our homes, ourselves. Many who, at the breaking out of the war, were in the first years of young manhood, are now in the full prime of their strength, and many of us who were then at the zenith of ripe manhood are now beyond the crest of the hill, and gray hairs and stooping forms admonish us that we are rapidly descending into the valley. Of the hundreds of men whose

names then appeared on the rolls of our regiment, and who entered the service with all the hope and ambition of true patriots, how few are with us to-day! Out of more than eighteen hundred names that appeared on our rolls during the time the regiment was in the service, but comparatively a small number survive to reap the benefits that their heroism and fidelity secured. The history of the regiment shows that it took part in 77 battles, besides numerous skirmishes. From Mechanicsville, where, on the 26th of June, 1862, it fired the first volley on the advancing enemy, to the final surrender at Appomatox Court House, it was almost constantly on duty.

When its three full years of service had expired, it was one of the few regiments that preserved its name and organization by re-enlisting in a body. The men who composed the Fourth Cavalry were not ready to depart for their homes even when their term of service had expired. They knew their country still needed them at the front, and although they could have returned to their homes with all honor, yet, like true patriots, like men who prized the interest of their imperilled country above all other considerations, they remained at the front, battling for the right, for the cause of humanity, for the integrity of the Union, until the last enemy of the country had thrown down his arms, and peace was declared throughout our wide domain. "Three years or during the war," was the services you agreed to render your country. But at the the expiration of that time, although you had stood every privation which fall to the lot of the soldier, you were still ready to try it for three years more. Thoughts of home were brushed aside along with the unbidden tear those thoughts were parent to, and you refused to listen to the pressing call of business, or social relation. The wants of your country were paramount to all else, and was the only consideration which impelled you to make the second sacrifice. Such lofty, such impartial patriotism is seldom to be found in any land.

But it is also proper that you should pause a moment in your season of conviviality, and think of those who have long since ceased to mingle with us here. Would to God I had the ability, the eloquence to speak of them in fitting terms. Would that I had the time, at least, to mention the name of

every hero of the regiment who gave his life to his country. But this I cannot do; and you must, therefore pardon me, if I refer to a few names only on the long death roll of our command. At Gaines' Mill on the 27th of June, 1862, when all was confusion and disorder, when the little valley that led down to the Chickahominy from Gaines' house, was filled with the dead and the dying, when our infantry broken and overpowered by the greatly superior numbers of the enemy, flushed with the hope of victory, came pressing over the crest of the hill like an irresistible torrent, at that fearful time when death reigned everywhere, do you remember who it was that stood at the head of his regiment like a statue, facing the storm as though it was a summer shower? It was the gallant, the noble Childs! He had been ordered by his superior officer to maintain a certain position, and that position he proposed to hold, or yield it only with his life. At Antietam —how I dread to name that place—that chivalric officer was taken from you. His conduct after he received the fatal wound was God-like. First he sent Captain Hughes, one of our honored citizens, who was on his staff, to General Pleasanton, and another of his aids to Lieutenant Colonel Kerr, to inform those officers that he was about to die, and to request them to see that his command was properly officered. He then sent word to the Surgeon to come to him, "if not attending to any one whose life could be saved, as he was in great pain." He then called his Adjutant, to whom he delivered his messages of love and affection for his family, and then, only forty minutes having elapsed since he received the fatal shot, he died. A braver and a better man never drew his sword in defense of his country. He was a man who could truthfully say: "I do love my country's good with a respect more tender, more holy, more profound, than my own life."

His life was nothing to him. It was a shadow compared with the interests of his country and his regiment.

And then you will all remember the gallant and intrepid Covode, who was at his post when duty called him, and ready for any emergency. What a splendid officer and gentleman he was! Genial, courteous, kind and generous when off duty, he was stern, yet dignified, brave, yet unassuming, when in the

face of the enemy. At St. Mary's Church, when shot down by a party of the enemy whom he believed to be his own men, his conduct was of the most heroic character. After receiving the fatal wound he was carried from the field, much . against his will. He wanted to confront the enemy as long as life lasted, and in the extremity of death he clung to his post. Such conduct is rarely to be witnessed, and for that reason the memory of the gallant Covode should be especially dear to us to-day.

At Farmville, on the 7th of April, 1865, the Fourth lost another of its most accomplished officers. He was one of our own boys—one of Venango's heroes. He was my personal warm-hearted friend, and I can hardly mention his name to-day, although so many years have passed, without profound emotion. But on the record of his regiment, on the pages of his country's history, on yonder marble shaft—wherever it is to be found—I know that you will agree with me when I say that in the whole history of the war there is not to be found a more honorable name than that of William B. Mays. Ah, me! when we think of the long list of our dead boys, how can we help feeling sad to-day? True, they died in a glorious cause. True, they were the preservers of their country. True, the brightest jewels in a martyr's crown are theirs. And equally true, I believe, the hand of God has inscribed the history of their priceless worth upon the records of a glorious eternity. But at the same time they were our brothers, our friends, our comrades. I would like to speak of all of them—officers and soldiers—of Kerr, Parke, Dunn, Say, Heckathorn, and oh, so many others; but it would be impossible on such an occasion.

Yes; we must leave our dead comrades; but as long as life lasts, in the quiet evening hour, in the stillness of the solemn night, in the rush and whirl of business, wherever we may be, the forms of our dead comrades will continue to pass before us, and as the years glide by those forms will become more and more distinct, as will the memory of our fallen comrades become dearer and dearer to each one of us.

Yes; ah, yes; on this day, when we are met together to renew old associations, it is eminently proper that we should

speak of our fallen braves. They have left a name of which the nation and humanity may well be proud; and their conduct has thrown a halo around the name of the Fourth Pennsylvania Cavalry which time itself can never obliterate. But while we would thus honor the dead, we should remember the living. Many are before me to-day who braved every danger of the battle-field, yet escaped without a scar. That they did so does not detract in the slightest degree from their record as true and valiant soldiers, but simply illustrates the mysterious way of Providence in permitting one to be taken and the other left. And, as we have already said, it is right that those who escaped should meet together, not only for the purpose of keeping alive and stimulating feelings of patriotism, but for the purpose also of keeping alive their organization. But a few only of these reunions can be had at best. Already the shadows are beginning to lengthen with many of us. Since your first meeting, there are many vacant chairs in the banquet hall. As year after year glides by, name after name will be stricken from the roll, and soon the last survivor of that regiment, which was an honor to the State, the County and the Nation, will pass away. For the few years then, that we can remain here, at best, let us preserve our identity as a regiment, and above all things let us preserve those feelings of friendship which should always exist between those who have shared dangers and privations together. If we will do this, then will our reunions be fraught with all that is desirable and praiseworthy, and a perfect absence of everything of an unpleasant character will pervade our midst. We will learn to think of and treat each other as brethren united by the most sacred ties. Then can we look forward with bright anticipations to each recurring anniversay of our organization. Yes, in my imagination, I see many happy reunions of our regiment in the future. Our numbers are growing less, but not our friendship and affection.

Appropriate addresses were also made by Col. Jno. S. McCalmont, Col. L. D. Rogers, of the Sixteenth Pennsylvania Cavalry. Capt. Mackey, Tenth Reserves, Capt. Hughes and Maj. W. N. Biddle, Fourth Pennsylvania Cavalry, after which the meeting adjourned.

GETTYSBURG MEETING.

A meeting of the Regiment was held at Gettysburg, Pa., October 6th, 1887, the purport of which is shown by the minutes :

GETTYSBURG, PA., October 6th, 1887.

In pursuance of notice published in the following papers, viz: Oil City Derrick, Oil City Blizzard, Franklin Evening News, Bethlehem Times, Eastern Express, Mauch Chunk Democrat, and three daily papers of Pottsville, a meeting of the surviving members of the Fourth Pennsylvania Cavalry was held at the Eagle Hotel, Gettysburg, October 6th, 1887, for the purpose of selecting a site for a monument, and appointing a committee to act in conjunction with the State Commission.

The meeting organized by electing Gen. W. E. Doster, President, and Maj. D. C. Phillips, Secretary.

On motion of Maj. Maitland, it was resolved that Gen. Doster, Maj. Maitland. Maj. Phillips, Capt. J. R. Grant and Capt. A. M. Beatty, be a committee of said regiment, to confer with the State Commission, for the purpose of taking advantage of the Act of Assembly of 1887, relating to appropriations for soldiers' monuments at Gettysburg.

On motion of Capt. J. R. Grant, it was resolved that the committee be empowered to select the design, the material and the inscription for said monument, and to contract for the erection of the same, under the powers given by said Act of Assembly; adding to the said appropriation such sum or sums of money as may be secured by the committee on subscriptions.

On motion it was unanimously resolved, that the monument be located on "the northwest corner of the Weikerd property; on the east side of Round Top Avenue," (stake No. 117).

On motion adjourned.   D. C. PHILLIPS, SECRETARY.

Immediately after the adjournment of the Regimental Meeting, the committee appointed to "select and erect the monument," met, and organized by electing Maj. J. B. Maitland, of Oil City, Chairman: Gen. W. E. Doster, of Bethlehem. Treasurer; and Maj. D. C. Phillips, of No. 68 Duquesne Way, Pittsburgh. Secretary.

On motion, the Secretary was requested to obtain suitable designs for submission to the committee, and the Chairman to prepare an inscription for like submission.

On motion, the following named persons were appointed a committee to solicit subscriptions, to be added to the appropriation from the State. All subscriptions to be handed or sent to the Treasurer, on or before January 1st, 1888.

GEN. W. E. DOSTER,	CAPT. J. R. GRANT,
MAJ. J. C. PAUL,	" A. A. PLUMMER,
" J. B. MAITLAND,	" W. K. LINEAWEAVER,
" J. P. BARR,	" A. M. BEATTY,
" D. C. PHILLIPS,	" D. C. BOGGS,
" R. J. PHIPPS,	LIEUT. A. B. WHITE,
CAPT. ALEX. FRAZIER,	" JAS. OGDEN.
" W. K. GILLESPIE,	

There being no further business, on motion, the committee adjourned to meet at the call of the Chairman.

D. C. PHILLIPS, SECRETARY.

THIRD REUNION,

AND

DEDICATION OF MONUMENT.

The third reunion was held at Gettysburg, on Pennsylvania Day, September 11th, 1889, upon the occasion of the dedication of the Monuments of the Pennsylvania organizations who participated in the battle of Gettysburg, the Fourth Cavalry being of the number. Transportation was furnished to its members entitled to the same, under the provisions of the Act approved May 8th, 1889. A business meeting was held in the Court House at 10 A. M., on September 11th, and the presence of our beloved Division and Brigade Commanders, Generals D. McM. Gregg and J. Irvin Gregg, aroused all to an intense spirit of enthusiasm, and their reception, amounting to an ovation, gave them additional proofs, if any were needed, of the devotion of the boys of the gallant Fourth to their trusted leaders, who had so many times led them to victory. The words of commendation from these men, as they briefly addressed us, were the best eulogy that the Regiment could desire. After arranging plans for the dedication of the monument, and placing the finances for its completion on a sound basis, adjourned to meet at the Camp-fire in the evening.

The Camp-fire was aglow ; and yet, pervading all, was a feeling of sadness, caused by the absence of many well remembered comrades, who have long since been mustered out,—some among the scenes of strife, others peacefully at their homes, surrounded by loved ones. The memory of all these was blessed, and we lovingly paid tribute to the worth of Welton, Covode, Childs and scores of others whose names and deeds are yet enshrined in our hearts. After an address of welcome by D. C. Phillips, Secretary, (see address), the following programme was, as far as possible, carried out, except the dedicatory address, which was delivered at the monument at 9 A. M., of Sept. 12th, and is appended hereto.

PROGRAMME.

FOURTH PENNSYLVANIA VETERAN CAVALRY REUNION,

AND DEDICATION OF MONUMENT,

GETTYSBURG, PENN'A., SEPTEMBER 11TH, 1889.

PRAYER—REV. D. CUPPS,   · · · · ·   Butler, Penn'a.

GREETING—MAJ. D. C. PHILLIPS, · · · ·   Pittsburgh, Penn'a.

SHEPHERDSTOWN—GEN. J. IRVIN GREGG, · Washington, D. C.

ST. MARY'S CHURCH—MAJOR J. C. PAUL, · · Chicago, Ills.

INCIDENTS OF ST. MARY'S CHURCH—

           SERG'T W. H. COLLINGWOOD, Pittsburgh, Penn'a.

FARMVILLE—MAJ. J. B. MAITLAND, · · · Oil City, Penn'a.

STONY CREEK—MAJ. J. P. BARR, · · · Grove City, Penn'a.

SAILOR'S CREEK—MAJ. J. R. GRANT, · · · Franklin, Penn'a.

GETTYSBURG—CAPT. A. M. BEATTY, · · · Dempseytown, Pa.

UPPERVILLE—LIEUT. COL. R. J. PHIPPS, · · Butler, Penn'a.

ANTIETAM—CAPT. ALFRED DARTE, JR., · · · Wilkesbarre, Penn'a.

CAMP LIFE—DOCTOR C. P. SEIP, ·. · · · Pittsburgh, Penn'a.

LIGHT DUTY—SURGEON F. A. BUSHEY, · · · Green Castle, Pa.

FORAGING—CAPT. W. K. GILLESPIE, · · · Pittsburgh, Penn'a.

LIBBY—LIEUT. A. B. WHITE, · · · · · Washington, D. C.

SULPHUR SPRINGS—LIEUT. C. S. MARK, · · Franklin, Penn'a.

PENINSULA—CAPT. CHAS. E. TAYLOR, · .· · Franklin, Penn'a.

APPOMATOX—GEN. S. B. M. YOUNG, · · · Ft. McIntosh, Tex.

OUR DEAD—CHAPLAIN H. Q. GRAHAM, · · · Homer City, Penn'a.

DEDICATORY ADDRESS—GEN. W. E. DOSTER, · Bethlehem, Penn'a.

Letters from absent comrades, expressing regrets and sending fraternal greetings, were read from Chaplain H. Q. Graham, Captain Wm. Hyndman, General S. B. M. Young, and others, followed by reading of paper on recovery of the body of Colonel Geo. H. Covode, then an address by Capt. A. M. Beatty, both of which are found herewith.

ADDRESS OF MAJ. D. C. PHILLIPS,

AT REUNION AT GETTYSBURG, SEPTEMBER 11, 1889.

COMRADES:—Notwithstanding my earnest request of your committee, that I should be excused from any attempt at speech making on this occasion (for, like our illustrious commander, Gen. Grant, I never made a speech in my life), they have assigned me the pleasant duty of welcoming you, veterans of the grand old Fourth Pennsylvania Cavalry, to this reunion, on this historic battle field of Gettysburg; a re-union, after more than a quarter of a century has passed since your gallant squadrons charged the enemies of your country, and drove them headlong from your native State.

No words of mine can adequately express the heart-felt pleasure it gives me to-night to look into the faces of so many of my old comrades, and to greet you with the warmest words of welcome.

But you have changed, greatly changed, since last we met. The hardships of those memorable years passed in the pines and swamps of Virginia, in camp, reconnoisance and battle, in Libby and Andersonville, sowed the seeds of disease and suffer-ing too plainly traceable on the countenances of many of those before me. These more than twenty-five years also, have done their part in changing the beardless boys of 1861 to 1865, into veterans, in appearance as well as reality.

Comrades—this reunion will be the last in which many of the veterans here assembled will take part. Cherish the friendships formed during those memorable years, which tried men's souls and nerves, when you stood shoulder to shoulder and hurled back the valiant but misguided foe.

Teach your children to reverence the flag you fought under : to preserve the liberties you fought for ; to defend, with their lives, if need be, the glorious union, which cost so much blood and treasure to preserve.

ADDRESS OF CAPT. A. M. BEATTY,

MR. PRESIDENT AND COMRADES:

I am happy to greet you on this historic field, and want to ask you to convene a court martial at once, as I have charges to prefer against two comrades. I had intended charging it to but one, and that was comrade Collingwood; but since comrade Maitland has told you that he had a hand in preparing the programme for this evening, I want to include him, and I hope you will find a verdict, and impose such a penalty that it will be an emphatic protest against such an imposition as inflicting me upon you for a speech at this time. I have no apology to make for my presence here on this field; I am here under orders, and do not deem an excuse any more necessary now than when I was here twenty-five years ago.

Gettysburg was, and is thought and said to be, one of the five decisive battles of the rebellion ; it was undoubtedly the most decisive, for here was defeated the best equipped and most powerful army the rebels ever had. They had made great preparations for the campaign before leaving home, and had acquired immense additions and strength in the way of supplies after coming into this great and loyal State. The old Keystone State, teeming with its millions of honest toilers was full to repletion. Its millions of bushels of grain, hundreds of thousands of horses and cattle, sheep, swine and poultry, was a vision to the eyes and a treat to the fiery veterans of Lee, whose military lives had most been spent on the exhausted soil and the wasted and worn sands of Virginia.

Their invasion was not a military necessity in the sense in which we are wont to speak of the moves of a campaign, but more of a political nature ; a movement born of desperation, and urged to force foreign recognition. It was undertaken with a full knowledge that it was to be a struggle to the death. Their conduct here, if it proves anything conclusively, proves that they fully realized this to be either the beginning of their success, or the beginning of the end.

Their conduct on this field has been sung in songs of praise throughout all the world during all the years of the quarter century ending to-day. That they fought heroically and bravely, none will deny. It would be belittling the courage and valor of our own troops for us to do so ; but with what mettle and what spirit were they met ? The army of the Potomac, well skilled in retreat, and fairly well taught in advancing, came winding its way from the banks of the Rappahannock, wearily toiling along the rugged foot hills and spurs of the Blue Ridge Mountains. Through a country already devastated and laid waste by the ruthless hand of war. It came, but a semblance of its former self, save in discipline and heroic determination to do or die, that the Union might live. And now I speak particularly of Pennsylvania soldiers, when I say that comrades, who under other circumstances, and on other fields, would have been laggards, vied not only with each other, but with those who always strove to be at the front, to reach the scene of carnage and to be on hand for the final struggle.

This spirit of determination and devotion was apparant throughout our whole army, and it seems as though it took just some such thing to arouse the Union army and its leaders to a sense of the importance of making a grand determined effort to prove to the whole world that this great Republic of the United States could regulate it own affairs, and take care of its own people, whether they were found following the paths of peace, or found in armed rebellion; and I take this opportunity to refute the idea and scout the sentimentalism which impels even some of our Northern speakers and writers to say, " that if we had failed and been defeated here, and they had won, the history of the rebellion would have been written the other way, and with the other hand." As soon expect the sun to come up at night. Never, since the advent of the Nazarene, has the progress of human rights gone backward ; nor the Scribe been long stayed whose hand has been engaged in enlarging the bill of human rights and human liberties.

Had we failed here and been crowded back into our own country, our homes and cities sacked, it would only have added

years and chapters to the history of the war, and have added generations to its victims.

No, only the base of operations would have been changed. The contest would have been waged in the hills and valleys of the Allegheny Mountains, or fought out in the vales and on the granite peaks of New England. For the principles involved, Humanity, guided and directed by Humanity's God, would have endured to the end.

But Providence spared us, and seemed to be with us, and the mantle of Fate seemed spread with her mystic hand over us. The selection of our main position was masterly generalship; while allowing it was a serious blunder. After its selection, the manner of attacking, and the three days of fighting, were a series of blunders on the part of the Rebel Commander; but with the strategy of the campaign I have nothing to do, and as little with the tactics.

Our own part in the battle, as the historian tells you, was a modest one, and all of you who were here will remember how surprised we were that our list of casualties was so small, placed as we were for three or four hours in direct range of eight or ten pieces of the enemies artillery stationed on either side of the Sharfy House.

It appeared to me like a storm of bursting shells and case shot, and I never remember of being under a cannonade, apparently so severe and destructive, which did so little damage. In many engagements—both before and after this one—which were insignificant in proportion, we lost heavily in horses and men from both artillery and small arms.

Whether it was our luck, or the fault of the Rebel artillerists, one can judge as well as another; but we were here to be shot if it was necessary, and I would remind my comrades of other commands that "it was not always the man who got shot the most that fought the most," and we will deny to-day that it was any fault of our own, and swear that we would have followed the gallant Doster wherever he would lead; that where he would not or could not lead, men could not go.

Yes, comrades, we were here inspired by that spirit of patriotism and love of country, which pervaded our whole army; and now we only ask recognition of the people of our common

country, in the same spirit which animated us then ; and ask them to remember their great anxiety least we would fail them at that time. Other fields of the war tell more of our powers in battle, but this one marks the greatest struggle of the war, and has been set apart by the great loyal hearts of our people as such, and designated as the Mecca of the patriot pilgrim, and the goal of the tourist.

This great forest of monuments, while in their individuality mark this place of acts of daring and heroism, and designate separate and distinct commands, as a whole teach an emphatic lesson and is an impressive lecture to all the young people of our country.

Many of you no doubt proudly claim, and justly so, lineal descent from the patriots and heroes of the American Revolution, and it has been, to many, a stimulus which urged them perhaps to greater deeds of daring and more steadfast devotion to the Union, and to the principles it embodies. They were grand men ; royal Americans, and the stars they planted in the azure field of our glorious national emblem, have shone with an undiminished lustre during all the years since, save the time they were obscured by the smoke of secession while borne by the columns breasting the waves of treason ; but our boast of Freedom and Liberty then was only an assertion, now, thank God, by your heroic devotion and sacrifices, it is a fact ; and as the record of your ancestors served its day and time as a talisman, urging you on to contest and victory, so let your history and achievements serve in guiding and directing the future of your children and children's children ; and if your pride of ancestry dates from the Revolution, its Lexington or Bunker Hill ; its Savannah or Yorktown, let the pedigree of your children start from the war for the suppression of the Rebellion : and let it date from Gettysburg, the hardest battle fought on Union soil, and the longest contested battle of the war.

Here, worn and weary, you met the foe elated with initial success and flushed with promised victory, and hurled them from Cemetery's bloody heights and Rebellion's highest mark, crushed and discomfitted : and without any disparagement of our leaders of that time, I will say that with Sheridan—the

27

Napoleon of American generals— here, they would have been annihilated, and never would have reached the south bank of the Potomac as an organization.

Our grand old army often suffered through its commander, although commanded by its best men. Historians, psychologists, and physiognomists, have all alike failed to explain why, nor will I attempt it now; but perhaps as rational an explanation as any can be found in the fact that many, amongst whom are to be found some of our loyal leaders who were gallant soldiers, profess to believe that the Rebels fought for what they believed to be right. I have stood on the sacred soil of this very field, no longer ago than last summer, and heard loyal Pennsylvanians slobbering over the Rebels assembled here, and telling them this. I have neither the time nor inclination to dispute or discuss this question, did I deem it neccessary, but will say the average Northern schoolboy of 14 years, or more, knows better. Now I hope you will pardon me for alluding to the politics of the war, and I will say nothing further on that point.

My recollections of the battle are those most deeply impressed on my mind, as on the average mind, by the most memorable events, and revert more particularly to sights and incidents connected with Pickett's charge. My post of observation was as near the summit of Little Round Top as safety of my person would allow, and was secured soon after the heavy artillery fire of the Rebels commenced, and maintained as long as anything could be seen through the darkness and the clouds and the canopy of smoke preceding darkness. Daylight was at a premium with us who were safe ; and all who were on the northeast side of Little Round Top, were comparatively so. They were secure from any direct fire during any time I was there. It was a grand sight, and a plain one, until about the time the Rebels' second line, or body struck the Emmettsburg road. It was accompanied by a field battery which was posted about two hundred yards west of the road, and by the time the battery got thoroughly to work their first line was hotly engaged with small arms. This, with the change of the position of the Vermont brigade, caused dense clouds of smoke to arise, which eddied overhead a little

south, although what air was moving was coming from the southwest. About this time we were practically shut out from view, and the artillery was about all that could be definitely located. I did not hear any express fears that the charge would be successful. Most of the comrades appeared to think, with an old Reserve man, who expressed himself that our artillery would do them up before enough of them reached our lines to accomplish anything effective. I don't say, for sure, that I formed or expressed any opinion of the charge at the time, so I can't say " I told you so." However, I believe I thought the effort would prove futile, for the report was credited that we had a large reserve of re-inforcements which had not been engaged, lying within supporting distance. I remember that we were all impressed with the gallant appearance of the Rebels and the brave manner in which they maintained their alignment and organization until after crossing the Emmettsburg road. Gaps and rents made in their ranks by our artillery were filled by other men as if those stricken down had dropped out in obedience to a command. But the same could not be said of them after crossing the road. It seemed to me that from there it was more a struggle to get inside our lines as a place of safety, than as a place to fight. More with a view to be taken than to take. Their experience coming over having taught them that to go back was certain death.

With the operations of our regiment after leaving the spot designated by our monument, I have no personal knowledge, further than the Taneytown road. All I know is hearsay, but as you did at other places and other fields, I know you did your duty, and went wherever ordered. In all that has ever been said about it, I don't think it could ever be truthfully said that we refused at any time or place, to go where ordered, or do our duty. Your attendance here proves that you are good to come when called. Allow me to congratulate you, one and all, on the success of our meeting, and hope that with all of you the time is not misspent ; that you will carry away pleasant recollections, renewed and strengthened affections.

29

AN INCIDENT OF THE BATTLE OF ST. MARY'S CHURCH.

BY W. H. COLLINGWOOD.

READ AT CAMP-FIRE, GETTYSBURG, SEPTEMBER 11th, 1889.

One of the most thrilling incidents in the history of the Regiment was the engagement at St. Mary's Church, which occurred on June 24th, 1864. The Fourth Pennsylvania Cavalry had been engaged in numerous battles, but there are circumstances and experiences which will probably fix the battle of St. Mary's Church indelibly in the memory of our surviving comrades.

The Second Division Cavalry Corps, Gen. D. McM. Gregg commanding, was vigorously attacked by the enemy, consisting of two divisions of cavalry and one of infantry. After a desperate encounter we retired, but each new position taken was flanked by the enemy. In this battle the Regiment lost in killed, wounded and missing, 87 men.

Among the killed, was our beloved and courageous Col. Geo. H. Covode. Several fruitless attempts were made to carry the body of our dying Colonel from the field. One was made by Serg't James Rankin, of Co. B. He was severely wounded and compelled to retire. Another was made by Capt. Geo. W. Wilson, Co. H.; Lieut. W. H. Slick, Co. D.; Joseph N. Tantlinger, Co. D., and several other members of the Regiment whose names cannot now be recalled, who placed the body on a litter made of rails and a blanket, and had retreated but a short distance when they too, were compelled to abandon the attempt and flee before the advancing enemy. Captain Wilson failed to make his escape and was felled by a blow from a Rebel musket, which broke several of his ribs. During the same day he made his escape and returned to the Regiment.

Darkness ended the contest. During the night the division retired and joined the cavalry corps the following evening, near Haxall's Landing, on the James' river.

The following day Gen. Sheridan crossed to the north side of the river. There we remained about two weeks.

30

About July 4th, Hon. John Covode, father of our lamented Colonel, visited our camp to learn the particulars of his son's death, and if possible to recover his body.

Lieutenant and Acting Adjutant J. C. Paul, called on Mr. Covode at Gen. J. Irvin Gregg's headquarters, and volunteered to enter the enemy's lines, and if possible secure the body of the Colonel. Gen. Gregg being present said he could not detail the lieutenant on such a dangerous journey as entering ing the enemy's lines, but would give him a letter to Gen. D. McM. Gregg, commanding the division.

The division commander in turn, gave Lieut. Paul a note addressed to Gen. Sheridan, asking that Lieut. Paul be permitted to go on his errand of love.

The Lieutenant being anxious to start on his journey after dark of the same day, and feeling sure that Gen. Sheridan would grant the request, detailed the following comrades to accompany him : Serg'ts Sam'l King, Co. L.; H. M. Kerr, Co. E., and Albert Martin, Co. D.

After reading Gen. Gregg's letter, Gen. Sheridan told Lieut. Paul he would not detail him to enter the enemy's lines, but would not prevent him if he so desired. The General also reminded the Lieutenant of the result in case of capture.

Lieut. Paul replied, that he and his comrades had weighed the matter well, and were willing to take all the risks.

"Then," said the General, "I will have a transport carry you across the river and remain there until you return, You can arrange a signal with the commander of the vessel to use in case you return during the night."

The party crossed the river after dark and started on their dangerous journey. The enemy's picket line was about eight miles from the river, the intervening space being neutral territory. The exact location of the picket line not being known, the detail under Lieut. Paul proceeded in a very cautious manner. Finally they saw the reflection of a fire apparently about a half mile in their front. Serg'ts King and Kerr dismounted, and taking to the woods on either side of the road, crawled the entire distance on their hands and knees.

31

They supposed the light to be at the Rebel picket reserve, and that the picket line must necessarily be in their immediate front. With this impression in mind they moved on slowly until they arrived near the fire. They found the fire was immediately in the rear of a temporary breast works, made by our division in the recent fight. Near the fire lay three "rebs," sound asleep. This was the enemy's outpost. Serg'ts King and Kerr did not disturb the watchful (?) sentinels, but hurried back and made their report to Lieut. Paul. The Sergeants offered to either kill or capture the three "Johnnies," but Lieut. Paul said "No; we will do nothing that may cause an alarm and interfere with our object." After a short consultation it was decided to retrace their steps. About a half a mile to the rear they took a road leading further to the left. In doing so they avoided the pickets which had been encountered. After going some distance inside the lines the squad headed for the main road again, and from that time on their pace was rapid. After proceeding three or four miles they found two of their wounded comrades in an old log hut which had been abandoned. The poor fellows had been there for nine or ten days, without attendance, and were unable to help themselves. Their wounds were filled with maggots, and they were in a most pitiable condition. They were put in as good shape as possible under the circumstances, furnished with food and water, and were promised they should be moved to the transport on the return of the squad. The promise was faithfully fulfilled. After leaving the wounded the party again pushed forward. As they advanced they found a number of dead comrades, unburied, but the time was so pressing that they could not inter the remains, much as they regretted to leave the bodies on the field. At last the squad arrived at a log cabin near which the Colonel's body had been left. They awoke the colored man who occupied the hut, and, after describing certain peculiarities of the Colonel, as well as his clothes, they inquired if he had seen the body and knew where it was buried ? The colored man, whose name is unfortunately unknown, took the members of the detail to the spot where Lieut. Paul remembered leaving the body. After procuring a lantern Lieut. Paul and those with him removed the

slight covering of earth and at once recognized Col. Covode's peculiarly formed teeth and his flannel shirt. The latter was of an odd pattern; the material having been made at his father's woolen mills, at Ligonier, Pa. The body was stripped of everything except the under clothing. After having identified the remains, the detail proceeded as far as St. Mary's Church, where they found two bodies within the building.

One poor fellow had died while endeavoring to crawl out, and lay in the doorway with his head on one arm, resting on the steps of the structure. The Lieutenant and his party then retraced their steps towards the river where they arrived shortly after daylight. The following night Lieut. Paul, with 30 picked men and two ambulances, returned for the Colonel's body. Leaving the ambulances in the woods about two miles to the left of the road, they proceeded with a litter, secured the body and again retraced their steps, arriving safely in camp the following forenoon.

The body now reposes in the grave yard in which the remains of his wife and parents rest, near Ligonier, Pa.

It is to be regretted that the only participants now remembered by the writer, of the detail of 30 comrades who finally secured the body of Col. Covode, are the following:

Capt. Wm. Hyndman, Co. A.
Capt. Frank H. Parke, Co. B.
D. R. Callen, Co. B, Allegheny.
Wm. Vantassell, Co. C, Apollo.
Henry Tillburg, Co. C, Williamsport, Pa.
John C. Walters, Co. C, Jamestown, N. Y.
Albert Martin, Co. D, Cedar Rapids, Ia.
Lieut. W. H. Slick, Co. D.
Robert Von, Co. D.
Jos. N. Tantlinger, Co. D.
Henry M. Kerr, Co. E, Boston, Pa.
Samuel King, Co. L.
James M. Bethaine, Co. I.
Loyal Adams, Co. L.

Lieut. John C. Paul, who figured so prominently in the recovery of the body of Col. Covode, was promoted to the position of Major of the Regiment for bravery on the field.

33

DEDICATION OF MONUMENT.

At 9 A. M., of September 12th, 1889, the Monument was dedicated, General W. E. Doster delivering the dedicatory address.

ADDRESS OF GEN. W. E. DOSTER.

Agreeably to the request of surviving comrades to write the history of our regiment during the Gettysburg campaign, and mindful of the necessity of attaining accuracy, I have consulted the regimental reports, made Aug. 4, Aug. 13, and Sept. 3, 1863, covering these operations, and on file in the War Department at Washington, and notes made by me at the time, and after comparing these with the recollection of other comrades, and visiting the field in 1882, 1886 and 1887, and conferring with Col. Bachelder, submit the following :

The part taken by the Fourth Pennsylvania Cavalry in this campaign, properly speaking, begins with the time when it formed a part of the Union Cavalry Corps of the Army of the Potomac, that encountered and held in check the Confederate Cavalry, through the passes in the Blue Mountains, south of the Potomac, while the infantry of both armies was passing northward toward Pennsylvania (a movement which covered the greater part of the month of June, 1863), and ends with the return of both armies to the line of the Rappahannock, near the end of July, 1863. During this period the Fourth Pennsylvania Cavalry was commanded by the writer, and formed part of the Third Brigade of the Second Division of the Cavalry Corps. The brigade was commanded by Col. J. Irvin Gregg, the division by Brig. Gen. D. McM. Gregg, and the corps by Maj. Gen. A. Pleasanton. In the same brigade with our regiment were the Sixteenth Pennsylvania Cavalry, Lieut. Col. J. K. Robinson ; First Maine, Lieut. Col. C. H. Smith ; Tenth New York, Maj. M. H. Avery. On the general staff were Captain, later Gen. Wesley Merritt, ambulance officer; and Captain, later Gen. Custer, the latter then already distinguished for his fighting on foot, in the advance, with his carbine. The three battalions of our regiment were com-

manded by Majors Covode, Biddle and Young. Co. A by Lieut. Joseph Andrews ; B, Capt. Frank H. Parke ; C, Capt. Robert D. Martin ; D, Capt. James T. Peale ; E, Capt. Robt. A. Robinson ; F, W. K. Lineaweaver ; G, Capt. Elias L. Gillespie ; H, Capt. Robert J. Phipps ; I, Lieut. Francis M. Ervay; K, Capt. James R. Grant ; L, Capt. Alender P. Duncan ; M. Capt. Alfred Dart, Jr.; Adjt. Lieut. A. B. White.

The campaign may be said to have been opened by the battle of Brandy Station, June 9th, 1863, a reconnoisance intended to ascertain whether the enemy was moving North. In this battle we formed a part of Gen. Duffie's division, which crossed at Beverly Ford, intending to effect a junction with Gen. Gregg's division which crossed at Kelly's Ford. During this action we were exposed to a severe artillery fire, and recrossed in the evening at Rappahannock Station. June 17 we were engaged at Aldie. June 18th we made a charge through the town of Middleburg and drove out the enemy, but finding the position untenable we retired from it at night. Next day, June 19th, we were ordered to retake the town, but, the enemy having been heavily reinforced, we found the task more difficult. Another charge followed, and we succeeded in dislodging them, and forcing them to take position about a mile west of the town, in a piece of woods, and behind the wall of a cemetery where they made an obstinate resistance. At last, by a united charge of our regiment and the First Maine, they were repulsed, and driven back to Upperville. June 20th we rested. June 21st we fought in the battle of Upperville, the account of which contained in the regimental report made Sept. 3d, 1863, is as follows :

HEADQUARTERS FOURTH PENNA. CAVALRY,)
September 3d, 1863.)

SIR :—I have the honor to report that on the morning of June 21st, I received orders from Col. Gregg to mount my regiment, which was encamped in the woods about one mile from Middleburg, on the Upperville road, and to move out in column of squadrons on the left of the Tenth New York and one battalion of the First Maine, on the right of the road leading to Upperville, which I accordingly did, moving at intervals from the protection of one knoll to another, until we had

advanced perhaps one mile, when my pioneer corps took possession of a small rifled gun which had been abandoned by the enemy in his flight. After proceeding about one mile farther I was ordered to cross the road and proceed parallel to it. This I did, at the same time deploying one company, dismounted, as skirmishers on my front, and afterward adding one squadron on my left. In this manner we reached a point within one-half mile of the town, occasional shots being exchanged between our skirmishers and those of the enemy. Here I was ordered to form my regiment as a support to and on the left of, I think, some regular regiments. Before the order to advance was given I was ordered to support Tidball's battery, then on the rising ground on the right of the road, in full view of the town and of the enemy.

After remaining here a short time I was ordered forward to the support of the battalion of the First Maine, which had been ordered to charge and drive the enemy from and beyond the town. I immediately ordered my regiment forward at a gallop, and after passing through and beyond the town some hundreds of yards, came up with the First Maine, which was formed on the road, apparently awaiting a charge by the enemy. In a few minutes the enemy * came dashing down the road, when I ordered my two first squadrons to advance carbines to be ready to receive them. The First Maine, after firing a few shots scattered to the right and left. The fire of my regiment being too hot for him, the enemy wheeled, and I ordered a charge, which was obeyed most promptly and gallantly by both officers and men. The enemy was driven from the field, leaving a number of killed, many wounded, and several prisoners in our hands. I then deployed two squadrons in the field on the right of the road as skirmishers, falling back some distance in the field with the principal part of my command. The enemy again charged, my men at the same time wheeling, so as to throw a flank fire into him as he passed along the road.

About twenty of my men then dashed into the road in his rear, and after a desperate hand-to-hand conflict, utterly routed and discomfited him, thus preventing his escape and

*Imboden and Robinson's Confederate Cavalry.

causing the capture of the entire party, variously estimated at from twenty to fifty men.

The division coming up at this time, it was impossible to give the exact number. I now received orders to rally my men and fall back beyond Upperville, where I encamped for the night. During the actions of the day the regiment sustained a loss of one killed, three severely wounded, one slightly wounded, and two taken prisoners. *

I am sir, very respectfully, your obedient servant,

W. E. DOSTER,

Lieut.-Col. Fourth Pennsylvania Cavalry.

To LIEUT. JOHN B. MAITLAND,

Act'g Asst. Adjt.-Gen. Third Cavalry Brigade.

The rest of the brigade was not engaged in the battle. †

On June 22d we retired from Upperville, ‡ through Middleburg to Aldie, with a strong rear guard, but there was no pursuit. On June 23d we marched to Leesburg, meeting a good deal of Union infantry marching in the same direction. June 24th, 25th and 26th, we were on picket at Goose Creek, with instructions to guard all roads leading to Edward's Ferry; and learned here that Lee was in Pennsylvania and Stuart behind us.

On June 27th we were ordered to fall back on the main body at Edward's Ferry, where we crossed the Potomac by a pontoon bridge in the evening, and reunited with the Army of the Potomac. The same night we pushed forward towards Frederick, Md,, but the night being dark the regiments and

---

* Official report, two killed, nine wounded, five missing—total sixteen.

† My brigade was not actually engaged in the battle of Upperville, on June 21st, except the 1st Maine and 4th Pennsylvania Cavalry, which was sent to the support of Gen. Kilpatrick in the afternoon. They charged the enemy repeatedly, driving him from town, and capturing one piece of artillery. Report of Col. J. Irvin Gregg.

‡ "We took two pieces of artillery, one being a Blakely gun, together with three caissons, besides blowing up one. We captured upwards of sixty prisoners, and more are coming in, including a Lieutenant Colonel, Major, and five other officers, besides a wounded Colonel, and a large number of wounded rebels in the town of Upperville. They left their dead and wounded upon the field. Of the former I saw upwards of twenty. We also took a large number of carbines, pistols and sabres. In fact, it was a most disastrous day for the rebel cavalry. Our loss has been very small both in men and horses. I never saw the troops behave better, or under more difficult circumstances." Report of Gen. Pleasanton.

brigades were all in confusion, and one-half of the Fourth strayed away. On Sunday morning, June 28th, we reached Jefferson, Md., and Frederick at 5 P. M., where the lost companies rejoined us. At Frederick we learned that Gen. Meade had superseded Gen. Hooker. On June 29th one of our men was killed in a brawl at Frederick. The same day we left Frederick and marched to Unionville. June 30th we passed through Westminister and camped near Manchester. On July 1st, at 5 o'clock in the morning, we reached Hanover, Pennsylvania; and slept in a wheat field. At 7 in the morning we were on the march again. Here we were told that Lee's army was at Gettysburg, that a battle had been fought, that Reynolds had been killed, and Howard was in command.

We arrived on the field at 11 o'clock, A. M., of July 2d, and encamped in a clover field on the Breiter farm, where White's Run crosses the Baltimore Pike. Soon after our arrival, about noon or early in the afternoon, I was detached from the brigade and ordered to report directly to Gen. Pleasanton with my regiment, at Gen. Meade's headquarters on the Taneytown road. On our arrival there, I was ordered by Gen. Pleasanton to go with a Captian of his staff and support some artillery. This officer guided us across rocks and fields, about half a mile from, and to the left of the army headquarters, and stationed us on rocky ground, with a clump of woods in our rear and artillery just in front, a short distance north of Little Round Top. Beyond the artillery was the Union infantry line. Our regiment was stationed by squadron front, partly in the woods. When we arrived the Union artillery was hotly engaged with the Confederate artillery posted on the opposing heights of Seminary Ridge, who had caught their aim well, and directed their fire upon us. † We stood exposed to this galling fire for several hours, during which time, the better to protect the men, I ordered them to dismount. None were killed, but many horses and men wounded. At last the staff officer who had placed us in position, relieved, and led us back

---

† "The enemy's guns, which had been brought up in large numbers, were wheeled into position and answered, and soon after, along all that ridge, where he had advantageously posted battery on battery, seemingly an interminable line, the fire was terrific, and the very air was filled with shot and bursting shells, like hail in the thick coming storm." S. P. Bates, Martial Deeds of Pennsylvania, pp. 259, second day of Gettysburg.

to headquarters. The ground we occupied, as since identified by Captains Grant, Beatty and other comrades, was on the northeast corner of the Weikerd farm, near the present Hancock Avenue. The clump of woods has since been cut down. It is to mark this spot that our monument is erected. On reaching headquarters the writer was invited to come into the farm house, and saw Gens. Meade, Butterfield and Pleasanton, sitting together in the inner room around a table. The latter remarked that there was no occasion for exposing the cavalry further, that Gen. Meade expected an attack on his right and rear, and that I should tell Gen. Gregg to keep a sharp look-out. I sent messengers to Gen. Gregg with this message and returned to the Breiter farm with the regiment, expecting to meet the division there, but no trace of it was left. It appears that at this time Gen. Gregg was skirmishing with the enemy about two miles east of Gettysburg, on the Hanover Pike, having with him the First and the rest of the Third Brigade. (See his report of July 25th, 1863.)

At 9 P. M. on the 2d, I was ordered to report again to Gen. Pleasanton, and under his personal superintendence, our regiment established a picket over the whole of the left of our line to the east of Gen. Meade's headquarters, and in advance of our infantry pickets, which we held until daybreak. We remained here on the reserve, a short distance south of the army headquarters on the Taneytown road, during the artillery duel between the two armies, until 2 P. M. of the 3d of July, when the enemy being reported advancing on the Littlestown road in our rear, I was ordered by Gen. Pleasanton to advance toward the right and hold them in check. Under these instructions we barricaded the Baltimore Pike and threw out a skirmish line, in which duty we were joined by the First Massachusetts Cavalry, under Lieut. Col. Curtis, who had similar orders.* Hearing cannonading to the north of us, we concluded that this was the attack we were ordered to meet, and marching in parallel columns with the First Massachusetts, we struck the Hanover Pike, where we found Gen.

---

* Col. Curtis, in a letter to me, dated July 16, 1886, says: "I remember very well that our two regiments were detached on the same duty July 3d, 1863, but regret that I cannot remember where it was that we were sent to look after a threatened attack on the right rear."

39

Gregg hotly engaged with Stuart's cavalry. The Rebel batteries got our range as we deployed into the orchard, just south of the present cavalry monument.†

On the night of the 3d of July we camped with the brigade between the Baltimore and Hanover Pike. On the 4th we stood in a pouring rain near Rummel's house. On the 5th we were ordered to advance to Gettysburg by way of the York road, and to wait at the cross roads of the York and Hanover Pikes for the rest of the brigade. As we advanced we found a Rebel picket line holding a piece of woods between us and the town. On our approach they surrendered and came into our lines. On this route we took possession of 5 hospitals and 300 wounded Confederates. At the junction of the York and Hanover Pike, in Gettysburg, we found a barricade across the street to the height of the second story of the houses, made up principally of wagons and furniture, which our pioner corps removed. Now began the pursuit of the fleeing army by way of Cashtown road or Chambersburg Pike. In the morning the Sixteenth had the advance. During the afternoon the Fourth held the advance, having one man killed by the rebel rear guard at Stevens' Furnace. On the 6th, at Fayetteville, we were ordered to advance toward Greencastle, and on this day the report shows we captured 100 rebels, 8 horses, destroyed 20 caissons and gun-carriages and a large quantity of ammunition and wagons. Ass't Adjt.-Gen. Maitland rode with us at times, urging us on. The movement was so rapid (frequently a gallop) that out of two hundred and fifty horses which we had when we left Gettysburg, only sixty were able to keep up when we reached Marion.* Here a citizen brought us word that Fitz-Hugh Lee's cavalry, numbering about 2000,

---

† "The 4th Penna. Cavalry, having been sent to report to Gen. Pleasanton, was not with me during July 3d, but joined me on the evening of that day, when my command was ordered to move to the front and take up a position on the left in order to meet a threatened attack in that direction. While remaining in that position the enemy got my range, etc." Report of Col. Gregg.

* June 30th, twenty-six officers and two hundred and seventy-eight men for duty. Record War Department.

"Near Marion I fell in with the rebel rear guard, under Fitz-Hugh Lee, and accordingly was ordered to fall back, rejoin the brigade and march to Chambersburg." Regimental report, Aug. 4, 1863.

"Continued the pursuit on the 6th to Marion, finding the road filled with broken down wagons, abandoned limbers and caissons filled with ammunition ready for immediate use. On July 7th, 8th and 9th were on the march from Chambersburg to Middletown, Md." Report of Col. Gregg.

were lying dismounted and unsaddled at Brown's Mills, in a field near by, which turned out, on examination by Capt. Duncan, to be correct. I sent back to the brigade for reinforcements, and suggested that now would be a favorable chance for an attack, and hid the remnant of the Fourth Pennsylvania Cavalry in the woods until the messenger returned. While waiting a citizen handed me a copy of the Philadelphia *Enquirer*, containing an account of the battle, and stating that the Potomac had risen and the Union cavalry had utterly routed the retreating army of Lee. When the messenger returned he reported, much to our surprise and regret, that my request for reinforcements was refused, and that I was ordered to fall back on the brigade at Fayetteville at once. We accordingly did so, and marched to Chambersburg, spiking one Rebel gun on our way back. †

On July 7th we marched with the brigade leisurely to Waynesboro' and Quincy. On July 8th we passed through Wolfsville and Myertown to Middletown, meeting Gen. Smith's force of militia. On July 9th and 10th we camped at Boonesborough, shoeing horses and laying in forage, rations and ammunition. On July 12th and 13th we received thirty-five new horses and were joined by Scott's nine hundred cavalry and detachments of the Thirteenth and Fourteenth Pennsylvania cavalry. On July 13th we rested. On July 14th we moved with Gregg's division, by a pontoon bridge, across the Potomac and camped that night on Bolivar Heights. What took place on the 15th of July is so fully told in the regimental report made at Sulphur Springs, Va., Aug. 13, 1863, that I copy the same entire :

SIR:—I have the honor to the report that immediately after the battle of Gettysburg and the pursuit of Lee as far as Marion (described in my last report), this regiment accompanied the brigade to Middletown and Boonesborough, Md., without any event of note occurring until July 14th, when the regiment recrossed the Potomac at Harper's Ferry and encamped on Bolivar Heights. On the 15th we marched with the brigade as far as Shepherdstown. About 4 P. M. was ordered by

41

Col. Gregg to advance four miles out the Winchester road to Wolper's Cross Roads and report my arrival. About one mile from Shepherdstown my advance guard encountered and drove before them a party of ten rebels, which was increased to about forty by the time I had reached the cross roads. They fled into the woods and renewed the attack, but were again dispersed.

I learned from a prisoner whom we captured that about five hundred rebel cavalry belonging to (A. G.) Jenkins, were at Leetown, in front; that a rebel cavalry force was on my left near Charlestown, and that a portion of Ewell's corps, whose drums were heard distinctly, was near Martinsburg and about three miles to my right, and sent the information to the Colonel commanding the brigade. I threw out pickets on all the roads and held them without further molestation until 11 P. M., when I was ordered back with three squadrons to Shepherdstown, the balance being relieved next morning. At 1 P. M. of the 16th, I was ordered to move my regiment on the right of the Winchester road and Randol's Battery, and instructed to support the battery while watching and holding the enemy in check on the right of the line. I successively advanced three squadrons—Captains Peale and Duncan and Lieut. Andrews—to the right of the line which became warmly engaged about 5 P. M., and so remained until the close of the day. Meanwhile two squadrons, Captains Peale's and Dart's, had been sent under Maj. Young to the support of the First Maine, and held their ground on the right of the road until orders were given to retire. Capt. Robinson remained as support of battery.

For gallant and meritorious conduct 1st Serg't John Harper, Company B, deserves special mention.

In this action seven were wounded and six missing.

I fell back with the brigade to Harper's Ferry the same evening and thence moved to Bristoe Station and Warrenton without meeting with anything unusual, except rest, rations and forage.

I am, very respectfully, your obedient servant,

W. E. DOSTER,
Lieut.-Col. Commanding.

LIEUT. MAITLAND, Ass't Adjt.-Gen.

42

On July 17th and 18th we were at Harper's Ferry, the infantry of the Army of the Potomac crossing the river at Berlin. On July 19th we marched by Leesburg, Warrenton Junction, Bristoe Station and Bealton to Amisville, where we arrived July 24th and resumed picketing, and patroling as far as Little Washington and Thornton's Gap. Lee was again on the Rapidan, and Meade on the line of the Rappahannock, and the Gettysburg campaign was over.

It will thus be seen that, in the month that elapsed between June 18th and July 18th, 1863, the Fourth Pennsylvania Cavalry was almost daily under fire, that it marched, in the course of that time, about five hundred miles; that it was among the foremost to assail the enemy's rear when he advanced and when he retreated; and in the actual shock of this great contest, it helped to stand the brunt in the centre of the line.

It is of course not within the scope of this address to give a history of this regiment from the time it was mustered into service, August 13th, 1861, to the time it was mustered out, July 1st, 1865. But it may appropriately be added, that it took part in seventy-seven battles and skirmishes, and lost in killed, wounded, died of disease or other causes, captured or missing, eight hundred and fifty-one, of which a record is kept, besides about one hundred of killed and wounded not recorded, making a total of nine hundred and fifty-one lost out of a total enlistment of nineteen hundred and thirty men, or about one-half. Thirteen of its commissioned officers were killed in action or died of wounds:—Col. James H. Childs, at Antietam; Col. George H. Covode, at St. Mary's Church; Maj. Wm. B. Mays, at Farmville ; Adj't J. E. B. Dalzell, at St. Mary's Church; Adj't Clement Engleman, at Dinwiddie C. H.; Adj't Jerome McBride, at Kelly's Ford ; Capt. Frank H. Parke, at Ream's Station; Capt. David P. Smith, at Poplar Grove Church; Lieut. John A. Welton, at Sailor's Creek; Capt. John C. Harper, at Hatcher's Run ; Lieut. Chas. E. Nugent, at Dinwiddie C. H.; Lieut. Francis W. Bowen, at Hawes' Shop, and Lieut. Alvin Youngs. Surely we, the survivors of that organization, may be proud that our names appear on the rolls of the Fourth Pennsylvania Cavalry, and that the monument dedicated here will keep its glory in perpetual remembrance.

43

After the ceremonies of dedication were over the members of the regiment readopted the Constitution and By-Laws of 1875 ; arranged for a reunion at Pittsburgh for September, 1890 ; elected officers ; appointed Secretaries for the different companies, with a view of securing a perfect roll and the addresses of surviving comrades ; then adjourned to meet at Pittsburgh. After which, assembling in front of the monument, a photograph of the regiment was taken, good-byes were said, and once more we left the battle scenes of Gettysburg, but with emotions quite different from those felt in 1863, when leaving the field of carnage.

It was a matter of mortification to the Committee that it was unable to present a completed monument, but delays occurred from time to time, beyond its control and that of our contractors, H. Oursler & Sons ; but the substance was there, and the imagination was left to supply the rest. On Friday, November 29th, 1889, the monument was formally accepted, on the part of the regiment, by A. M. Beatty and J. B. Maitland ; and for the State, by the Commission. It is a matter for congratulation that the regiment received the recognition it merited in the occupancy of the site on which the monument is erected, and that, in the monument itself, it has an enduring fame, second only to its magnificent achievements.

The monument is of Westerly granite, bearing on its front the figure of a soldier, mounted, and the names of the regiment, brigade and division ; on the other side the legend :

DETACHED ON THE MORNING OF JULY 2ND, FROM THE BRIGADE AT THE
JUNCTION OF WHITE RUN AND BALTIMORE TURNPIKE, ORDERED TO
REPORT TO HEAD QUARTERS, ARMY OF THE POTOMAC,
SUPPORTED A BATTERY TEMPORARILY NEAR THIS POSITION,
ON PICKET AT NIGHT, RETURNING LATE ON THE AFTERNOON OF THE 3RD TO
SECOND CAVALRY DIVISION
MUSTERED IN AUG. 15 TO OCT. 30 1861 RE-ENLISTED JAN. 1 1864
MUSTERED OUT JULY 1 1865
RECRUITED IN NORTHAMPTON ALLEGHENY WESTMORELAND INDIANA
VENANGO LEBANON AND LUZERNE COUNTIES
TOTAL ENROLLMENT 1930

KILLED AND DIED OF WOUNDS OFFICERS	9	MEN 92	TOTAL 101	
DIED OF DISEASE ETC.	"	3	" 252	" 255
WOUNDED	"	21	" 248	" 269
CAPTURED OR MISSING	"	5	" 266	" 271

TOTAL CASUALTIES 896

FROM MECHANICSVILLE JUNE 26 1862
To
APPOMATTOX APRIL 9 1865.

44

DIMENSIONS OF MONUMENT.

First Base......................9:0 x 4:6 x 1:6.
Second Base....................8:0 x 3:6 x 1:3.
Die............................7:0 x 8:0 x 2:0.
Height.........................10:9.
Weight.........................38,440 lbs.

Comrades should make Gettysburg their Mecca, and those who have not made the pilgrimage are recommended to make it, and see, for themselves, one of the finest monuments on the field, commemorating the deeds of valor of a regiment justly proud of its record.

Your Publishing Committee deem it but just that the services of the Committee having in charge the erection of the monument at Gettysburg, should receive proper recognition, take this means of acquainting the regiment at large of the work accomplished at great personal inconvenience, time and expense; going again, and again, to the battle field, and to other places, in securing a site, and carrying forward to completion the enterprise undertaken. We wish, furthermore, to congratulate the regiment that it has a monument completed and paid for, which is in all respects an honor to it, as well as to the Committee who so faithfully performed the arduous labors in connection with planning and erecting it; the total cost of which was about twenty-five hundred ($2,500.00) dollars, fifteen hundred dollars being appropriated by the State, and balance, one thousand dollars, was contributed by comrades and their friends.

In order to have as complete a record as possible of the surviving members of the Fourth Pennsylvania Cavalry, comrades are earnestly requested to send name and address of any member not found in the following List, to the Corresponding Secretary, Wm. H. Collingwood, 715 Liberty Street, Pittsburgh, Pa.

45

LIST OF SURVIVING MEMBERS

OF THE FOURTH PENNSYLVANIA CAVALRY, INCLUDING
THOSE WHO WERE PRESENT AT DEDICATION OF
MONUMENT, GETTYSBURG, SEPT. 12, 1889.

NAME.	COMPANY.	POST-OFFICE.	
John H. Ashbaugh	D	Hillsview, -	Penn'a.
L. J. Adams	M	Carbondale,	"
George R. Berry	M	Gilatt, -	"
Jeremiah Brinker	C	Latrobe, -	"
John Broadback	A	South Easton,	"
John Boyce	B	Pittsburgh,	"
Wm. C. Bigler	K	Cranberry, -	"
William Blake	D	Irwin Station,	"
Henry Bender	I	Wallaceville,	"
H. F. Bowman	H	Neilsburg, -	"
Geo. W. Brown	B	Economy, -	"
John H. Beckman	D	New Florence,	"
Absalom Bumgardner	H	Witherup, -	"
Andrew Brown	H	Grapeville, -	"
Maj. John P. Barr	L	Grove City, -	"
John Barber	C	Paulton, -	"
James F. Billingsley	K	Utica, -	"
Capt. A. M. Beatty	H	Dempseytown,	"
Sylvester J. Brandon	L	Coal City, -	"
Dr. William G. Bishop	L	Brookville, -	"
S. C. Bole	E	Leechburg, -	"
James M. Bethune	I	Knox, -	"
Ass't Sur. Frank A. Bushey		Greencastle,	"
Wm. J. Boyd	A	Mauch Chunk,	"
Henry M. Black	K	Duke Centre,	"
Frederick Berge	M	Scranton, -	"
T. C. Byrnes	I	Cranberry, -	"
J. W. Baker	K	Millbrook, -	"
abana S. Cline	E	Leechburg, -	"

NAME.	COMPANY.	POST-OFFICE.
R. C. Sgt., W. H. Collingwood,	E	Pittsburgh, - Penn'a.
Benj. Cable	D	Bolivar, - "
James Caldwell ..	D	Brinton, - "
Alexander Campsey	A	E. Mauch Chunk. "
Robert P. Clark	H	Lottsville, - "
Geo. W. Conrad	M	Glenwood, - "
Wm. Cruikshank	B	Verona, - "
M. B. Conrad	M	Carbondale, - "
R. B. Crawford	L	Tionesta, - "
Lodovic Conrad	M	South Gibson, "
Geo. W. Crawford	B	Dixmont, - "
John Caldwell	G	Pittsburgh, - "
Hugh Crawford	B	Canton, - "
L. B. Caushey,	C	Penn Station, "
D. R. Callen	B	Allegheny, - "
Harrison Craig	B	Pittsburgh, - "
David Cupps	E	Butler, - "
John Daywalt	C	Mercersburg, "
W. H. Devenney	I	Franklin, - "
James S. Duncan	C	East Sandy, "
Capt. Alfred Darte, Jr.	M	Wilkes-Barre, "
Robert Dickinson	E	Hopewell, - "
James R. Downing	H	Seneca, - "
Geo. H. Dull	E	Fayette City, . "
Wm. H. Durning	I	Franklin, - "
Thomas M. Dias	E	Elizabeth, - "
Josephus Dick	E	Camden, - "
Wm. W. Dunbar	G	Evans City, - "
Absalom Darkes	F	Conshohocken, "
Geo. A. Dewoody	H	Balliet. - "
David W. Davidson	L	Sunville, - "
John Dempster	E	Irwin, - "
L. C. Darte	M	Wilkes-Barre, "
Abner N. Darte	M	Tirzah, - "
Wm. Duncan	E	Uniontown, - "
Gen. W. E. Doster	A	Bethlehem, - "
John A. Ebright	F	Lebanon, - "
T. J. Edwards	A	Mahanoy City, "

NAME.	COMPANY.	POST-OFFICE.	
John T. Ewens	I	Pittsburgh, -	Penn'a.
Charles O. Ellis	M	Waymart, -	"
R. B. Fraser	A	Pittsburgh, -	"
Geo. Franzy	C	Dubois, -	"
Nathan Fritz	A	Ashley, -	"
Alexander T. Felton	M	Carbondale,	"
Capt. Alex. Frazier	I	Cooperstown,	"
Wm. M. Gayetty	H	Venus, -	"
Dr. John J. Green	C	Pittsburgh, -	"
Condy. Gallagher	A	Lansford, -	"
Geo. Ghearing	I	Dempseytown,	"
Chaplain, H. Q. Graham		Homer City,	"
John Boyd Galy	L	Seneca, -	"
Capt. Wm. K. Gillespie	E	Pittsburgh, -	"
David R. P. Gates	K	Knox, -	"
Capt. J. R. Grant	K	Franklin, -	"
Wm. Gamble	F	Lancaster, -	"
Geo. K. Hess	F	Lebanon, -	"
S. P. Heath	E	Boston, -	"
Robt. A. Hutchinson	L	Kennerdell, -	"
Sam'l Hull	D	New Florence,	"
Wm. G. Hall	H	Cooperstown,	"
Lieut. John B. Hogue	I	New Lebanon,	"
James Hoover	I	Cooperstown,	"
Geo. Hoon	D	Ligonier, -	"
R. M. Hoffman	K	Kennerdell, -	"
J. N. Hoskinson	D	Bolivar, -	"
Herman J. Hambleton	F	Philadelphia,	"
Frederick Imhof	F		
John Irvin	B	Allegheny, -	"
Cal. James	I	Oil City, -	"
Geo. F. Joslin	M	Wilkes-Barre,	"
David Jones	E	Allegheny, -	"
Henry M. Kerr	E	Boston, -	"
James R. Knox	D	Manhattan, -	Kansas.
Geo. W. King	K	Franklin, -	Penn'a.
Geo. B. Kent	A	Summit Hill,	"
John D. Kirkpatrick	B	Allegheny, -	"

NAME.	COMPANY.	POST OFFICE.
Chas. C. Kirchner	C	Latrobe, - Penn'a.
Wm. Kain	A	Walnutport, "
Reuben H. Kieffer	F	Annville, - "
John Lichtenfelt	D	Bolivar, - "
Thomas Lockwood	E	Greenoch, - "
John Lamb	E	Boston, - "
Jacob Lyons	H	Franklin, - "
James Little	K	Service, - "
John H. Leasher	C	Pleasant Unity, "
Samuel Lowry	F	Bismark, - "
Peter P. Lafever	G	Livermore, - "
Michael J. Murphy	M	Beaver Falls, "
Daniel McCarthey	C	Latrobe, - "
Joseph Mooreland	B	New Wilmington, "
Jno. P. Maitland	L	North Clarendon, "
Lieut. James A. Morrison	E	Branchton, - "
John H. Matthews	F	Myerstown, "
Isaac Maloney	H	Polk, - - "
Capt. Geo. W. Moss	F	Wilkes-Barre, "
Abram S. Martin	E	Locust Lane, "
Lieut. Cyrus S. Mark	I	Franklin, - "
A. T. Malin	C	Robbins Station, "
Maj. J. B. Maitland	L	Oil City, - "
Robt. H. McMunn	B	Allegheny, - "
John T. Murdock	G	Allegheny, - "
John W. Moore	G	Pittsburgh, - "
David L. Miller	H	Franklin, - "
Samuel H. Murray	D	Creek Side, - "
Sam'l Miller, Nat. Mil. Home,	C	Milwaukee, - Wis.
Geo. H. Nez	C	Connellsville, Penn'a.
James Ogden	D	Latrobe, - "
Surgeon W. B. Price		Berlin, - Ills.
John Poorman	M	Middletown, Penn'a.
Levi Porter	K	Clintonville, "
Robert M. Painter	E	Elizabeth, - "
James A. Painter	E	Manor Station, "
S. F. Karnes	L	Canonsburg, "
Daniel Kiester	K	Franklin, - "

NAME.	COMPANY.	POST OFFICE.
Lieut. Abner J. Pryor	L	Rockland, - Penn'a.
Maj. Duncan C. Phillips	F	Pittsburgh, - "
Lieut. Col. Rob't J. Phipps	H	Clintonville, " -
James Patton	E	Elizabeth, - "
John Quinn	G	Pittsburgh, - "
Isaac Robbins	E	Philadelphia, "
Lieut. Jos. W. Russell	K	Grove City, "
David H. Rayzor	K	Barkeyville, "
Henry Raizer	F	Lebanon, - "
David Ray	H	Cooperstown, "
John G. Robison	D	West Fairfield, "
A. W. Robertson	H	Cooperstown, "
John Rinker	A	Leighton, - "
Philip Raiger	F	Reading, - "
Isaac J. Robb	D	New Florence, "
Samuel E. Reynolds	B	Allegheny, - "
Albert R. Sloan	K	Eldred, - "
Geo. Schlager	A	Scranton, - "
W. J. Stewart	G	Sewickley, - "
Thos. S. Speakman	E	Joint, - "
Wm. A. Seaton	L	Forestville, - "
Absalom Shuler	K	Hilliards, - "
Geo. W. Spealman	E	Apollo, - "
A. G. Sollinger	L	Canonsburg, "
Josiah H. Seabold	F	Annville, - "
David Scully	D	Laughlinstown, "
Charles S. Sanford	H	East Smethport, "
J. B. Snyder	L	Franklin, - "
Rufus P. Seely	I	Wallaceville, "
Dan. Sollinger	L	Rockland, - "
Dr. C. P. Seip.	B	Pittsburgh, - "
Lieut. Wm. H. Slick	D	New Florence, "
John Sorby	B	Verona, - "
John L. Stouffer	C	Greensburg, "
Sam'l Stouffer	C	Greensburg, "
Edward Stroup	I	Tidioute, - "
Wm. Stermer	A	Mauch Chunk, "
Wm. G. Sheppard	L	Porterfield, - "

NAME.	COMPANY.	POST-OFFICE.
Daniel W. Servey	I	Curllsville, - Penn'a.
W. B. Sheilds..	D	
Marlin T. Thompson	C	Pittsburgh, - -"
Abraham T. Taylor	L	Bradford, - "
Joseph N. Tantlinger	D	West Fairfield, "
Nelson M. Thompson	E	Apollo, - "
Chas. H. Tripp	H	Evansburg, - "
Henry Tilburg	C	Montgomery, "
John H. Ulrich	F	Annville, - "
J. Vandermark	M	Carbondale, - "
Vet. Sur., Jas. A. Van Horn	B	Hunlocks Creek, "
W. H. Vantassel	C	Apollo, - "
Sharpless Wise	K	Franklin, - "
John B. Woodling	K	Jackson Centre, "
Lieut. Geo. W. Wise	K	Callensburg, "
Lee M. Wilson	B	Murdocksville, "
Jacob S. Wikel	F	Hummellstown, "
Samuel M. West	C	Apollo, - "
James Wilkins	H	East Green, - "
Thomas J. Watt	I	Wallaceville, "
William Wright	C	Pittsburgh, -. "
John W. Welsh	A	Weissport, - "
Charles T. Yoder	C	Washington, D. C.
John B. Yost	A	Hazelton, - Penn'a.
Gen. S. B. M. Young	B	Ft. McIntosh, Texas.
Maj. Jas. T. Peale	D	Washington, D. C.
Maj. Jno. C. Paul	C	New York City, N. Y.
Maj. J. H. Trimble		McKeesport, Penn'a.
Capt. A. A. Plumer	I	Franklin, - "
Lieut. Geo. C. Morton	B	East Liverpool, Ohio.
Ass't Surg., J. S. Skeeles.		Albion, - Penn'a.
R. Q. M. Sgt., G. M. Bacon.	G	Greensburg, "
Capt. Wm. Hyndman	A	New York City, N. Y.
Hosp. Stew., John Fulton	G	New York City, N. Y.
Rob't Crawford	A	Mauch Chunk, Penn'a.
Rob't Boston	A	Humboldt, - "
John Drumbore	A	Lehighton, - "
John S. Webb	A	Lehighton, - "

NAME.	COMPANY.	POST-OFFICE.	
Andrew Graver	A	Weissport, -	Penn'a.
Reuben Arner	A	Weissport, -	"
John Lewis	A	Coaldale, -	"
Chas. Kech	A	E. Mauch Chunk,	"
W. F. McClure	A	Kester, -	Col.
Jos. McLaughlin	A	Summit Hill,	Penn'a.
J. Katzmoyer	A	Summit Hill,	"
James. Davis	A	Summit Hill,	"
J. E. Richards	A	Lansford -	"
John Jeffries	A	Lansford, -	"
Edwin Gwlym	A	Lansford, -	"
A Kettra	A	Lansford, -	"
Tilman H. Ash	A	Wilkes-Barre,	"
Henry J. Miller	A	Oil City, -	"
Capt. Jas. H. Grenet	B	Pittsburgh, -	"
Thos. Cruikshank	B	Verona, -	"
Jas. Zollinger	B	Pittsburgh, -	"
Geo. W. Speer	B	Allegheny, -	"
Alfred Masonhimer	B	Allegheny, -	"
Hugh Handlon	B	Pittsburgh, -	"
A. F. Scott	B	Allegheny, -	"
Phil. Zollars	B	Allegheny, -	"
Lawrence Hinnure	B	Chartiers, -	"
Michael Solar	B	Allegheny, -	"
Alonzo Harpending	B	Waterloo, -	N. Y.
Geo. Stedeford	B	Allegheny, -	Penn'a.
Jas. S. Phillips	B	Pittsburgh, E. E.,	"
John W. Cassidy	B	Pittsburgh, -	"
Thos. L. Davis	B	Finleyville, -	"
H. J. Blaisdell	C	Oakdale, -	Fla.
Michael Bash	C	Apollo, -	Penn'a.
Uriah Neptial	C	Apollo, -	"
Isaac Barber	C	Apollo, -	"
Lieut. Wm. A. Thompson	C	Pittsburgh, E. E.,	"
John G. Frederick	C	Irwin Station,	"
Isaac Miller	C	Parker's Landing,	"
Andrew Hice	C	Pittsburgh, E. E.,	"
Dr. W. A. Sanders	C	Braddock, -	"

NAME.	COMPANY.	POST-OFFICE.
Daniel McCadden	C	Livermore, - Penn'a.
Isaac Blackson	C	Pleasant Unity, "
N. Brindenthall	C	Latrobe, - "
D. L. Crawford	C	Latrobe, - "
Wm. Sindorf	C	Derry, - "
John McGuire	C	Livermore, - "
H. B. Simons	C	Red Cloud, - Neb.
James Kilgore	C	Pittsburgh, - Penn'a.
A. S. Marshall	C	Clarksburg, - "
Daniel Kelly	C	Greensburg, - "
H. L. Freeby	C	Tawas City, - Mich.
J. M. George	C	Philipsburg, Penn'a.
Lieut. A. W. Martin	D	Cedar Rapids, Iowa.
Peter Winebriner	D	New Florence, Penn'a.
Wm. P. Ferguson	D	New Florence, "
Michael McCullough	D	New Florence, "
Tobias W. France	D	Bolivar, - "
Wilson P. France	D	Bolivar, - "
Reuben Reed	D	Dunbar, - "
R. J. Smith	D	Wooster, - Ohio.
James Caldwell	D	Brinton, - Penn'a.
Matt. W. Brown	D	West Fairfield, "
D. J. C. Peer	D	West Fairfield, "
Alex. Irwin	D	Hillside, - "
Henry C. Wakefield	D	Seward, - "
David S. Wakefield	D	Seward, - "
James R. Long	D	Seward, - "
Isaac Johns	D	Seward, - "
Israel Johns	D	Seward, - "
Samuel D. Murphy	D	Ligonier, - "
Thomas Hill	D	Altoona, - "
William McDowell	D	Altoona, - "
Joseph Fry	D	Bottsville, - "
Adam Mangus	D	Hillsview, - "
W. D. Blackburn	D	Washington, D. C.
Thos. Walker	D	Greensburg, - Penn'a.
Geo. W. Beistel	D	Ligonier, - "
John A. Baker	D	Ligonier, - "

NAME.	COMPANY.	POST-OFFICE.
Isaac Sarena	D	Ligonier, - Penn'a.
James Shrum.	D	Ligonier, - "
John A. Wherry....	D	Pittsburgh, - "
Capt. A. F. Coon	E	David City, - Neb.
Hon. Martin A. Foran	E	Cleveland, - Ohio.
David Spealman....	E	Brush Valley, Penn'a.
Daniel Fouks	E	Penn Station, "
Wm. Marhoff	E	Greenoch, - "
J. C. O'Brien	E	Medina, - Minn.
Alex. Gregg...	E	Salem, - Penn'a.
Geo. H. Tiel....	E	Laughlinstown, "
Jas. M. McLaughlin	E	Helena, - Mont.
Allen Foster	E	Brush Creek, Iowa.
Wm. D. Smith	E	Medina, P. O., Minn.
John G. Smith	E	Irwin, - Penn'a.
S. Fry	E	Irwin, - "
John A. Fulton	E	Sabetha, - Kan.
Geo. B. Hays	E	Kanawha Sta'n, W.Va.
Wm. Leck...	E	Vesta, John'n Co. Neb.
Benj. Thomas, Sol. Nat. Home,	E	Milwaukee, - Wis.
James Clark	E	New Florence, Penn'a.
Robt. Mack.	E	Clyde P. O., - "
Joseph Gillespie	E	Esdaile, Pierce Co.Wis.
Wm. R. Johns...	E	New Florence, Penn'a.
David R. P. Mann	E	Homestead, - "
Theo. Deuring	E	Cincinnati, - Ohio.
Jas. Scannell	E	Germantown, "
Lieut. A. B. White	F	Washington, D. C.
Capt. W. K. Lineweaver	F	Pottsville, - Penn'a.
Maj. Daniel C. Boggs	G	Stuart, - Neb.
Lieut. Alex. Matchett	G	Pittsburgh, - Penn'a.
Lieut. B. C. Adams	G	Pittsburgh. - "
P. F. McCloskey	G	East Liverpool, Ohio.
A. Morrison, Sol. Nat. Home,	G	Dayton, - "
F. Haviland, " " "	G	Dayton, - "
Robert Osborn....	G	Chicago, - Ills.
N. C. Stevenson	G	Mt. Chestnut, Penn'a.
Robert T. Crawford	G	Benzonia, - Mich.

NAME.	COMPANY.	POST-OFFICE.	
Thomas Aiken	G	Allegheny, -	Penn'a.
W. D. Foote	G	Mattoon, -	Ills.
B. M. Duncan	G	Butler, -	Penn'a.
A. M. Borland	G	Butler, -	"
Wm. Barr	G	Beaver Falls,	"
Alfred Dunbar	G	Evans City, -	"
Alpheus Dunbar	G	Evans City, -	"
R. D. Stoller	G	Wilkinsburg,	"
I. N. Duncan	G	Butter Cupps,	"
Anthony Chambers	G	Pittsburgh, -	"
E. G. Duncan	G	Greenfield, -	Iowa.
Hiles Fleeger	G	Fleeger, -	Penn'a.
Eli S. Fleeger	G	Fleeger, -	"
Hammond Gardner	G		- "
Samuel Irvin	G	Butler, -	"
Hugh Miller	G	Parkers Landing,	"
John Miller	G	Zelienople, -	"
Henry Miller	G	Harmony, -	"
Josiah McKissock	G	Edenburg, -	"
Edward Randolph	G	Zelienople, -	"
Samuel Seaton	G	Boyer P. O.,	"
J. H. Shannon	G	Allegheny, -	"
John Watters	G	Evans City, -	"
Samuel Miller	G	Butler, -	"
Capt. Andrew Nellis	G	South West City,	Mo.
A. G. Wilkins	H	Meadville, -	Penn'a.
Asa Clark	H	Blooming Valley,	"
Harvey A. Hatch	H	Blooming Valley,	"
J. M. Gayetty	H	Oil City, -	"
Hiram Connor	H	Franklin, -	"
E. Dewoody	H	Franklin, -	"
William Brown	H	Cooperstown,	"
J. R. Stover	H	Fertig P. O., -	"
Matt. B. Connor	H	Bridgeville, -	"
Caleb Gray	H		- "
Geo. W. Lindly	H		- "
Cyrus Michael	H		- "
W. H. Varner	H		- "

NAME.	COMPANY.	POST OFFICE.	
Walter C. Parker	H	Reynolds, -	Neb.
Capt. Geo. W. Wilson	H	Cranberry,	Penn'a.
Chris. Hyser	H	McDonald, -	"
Chas. W. McElravy	H	Reidsburg, -	"
Capt. Charles E. Taylor	I	Franklin, -	"
B. F. Crain	I	Utica, -	"
Robt. Hilands	I	Franklin, -	"
James Dille	I	Cooperstown,	"
Robt. J. McClelland	I	Cooperstown,	"
Daniel J. Brown	I	Waterford P. O.	"
A. W. Kinnear	I	Raymilton "	"
Barnett Lupher	I	Canal "	".
J. Randall	I	Franklin, -	"
D. Z. McCracken	I	Franklin, -	"
W. Tarr	I	Cherry Tree P. O.	"
S. M. Lupher	I	Canal P. O.,	"
Crawford Belig	I	Sunville P. O.,	"
Geo. Leslie	I	Kossuth "	"
John Vorous	I	New Lebanon,	"
Wm. Strite	I	New Vernon,	"
John Findley	I	Clark's Mills,	"
F. R. Showalter	I	Grafton, -	Ohio.
J. L. McCalmont	I	Chardon P. O.,	Penn'a.
William Reagle	I	Raymilton, -	"
Al. H. Jackson	I	Cooperstown,	"
Lewis Byers	I	Sonora P. O.,	"
Geo. Kinnear	I	Raymilton,	"
M. F. Hasson	I	Centerburg,	Ohio.
Wm. H. Thompson	I	Ottumwa, -	Iowa.
Wm. B. Keener	I	Silver Cliff, -	Col.
Silas L. Davis	I	Pittsburgh, -	Penn'a.
Capt. Francis M. Ervay	I	Dallas, -	Texas.
Jacob Harlan	K	Balliet P. O.,	Penn'a.
Robert Shaw	K	Barkeyville,	"
William Hackett	K	Franklin, -	"
H. Moyer	K	Balliet P. O.,	"
Jonathan McKean	K	Crawfords Corner,	"
A. W. Shorts	K	Franklin, -	"

NAME.	COMPANY.	POST-OFFICE.
S. R. Weston	K	Wesley P. O. Penn'a.
Eli Hovis	K	Clintonville, "
Thomas McLaw	K	Polk P. O., - "
J. H. Montjar	K	Clintonville, "
Benj. Stover	K	Emlenton, - "
Solomon Funk	K	Findley, Hanc'k Co.,O.
M. V. Phipps	K	Wesley P. O. Penn'a.
A. J. Phipps	K	Wesley " "
Israel S. Yard	K	Barkeyville, "
Alvey Bigley	K	Barkeyville, "
Jos. Bleakley	K	Barkeyville, "
Jas. Bleakley	K	Barkeyville, "
A. M. Jones	K	Barkeyville, "
Robt. S. Sarver	K	Franklin, - "
W. B. Foster	K	Franklin, - "
J. R. Dodds	K	Polk P. O., - "
P. S. Atwell	K	Big Bend P. O., "
R. M. Hovis	K	Clintonville, "
Perry McFadden	K	Kennerdell P. O., "
W. W. Crawford	K	Clintonville, "
Jacob Henderson	K	Balliet P. O., "
Robert Shorts	K	Kennerdell, - "
L. Sauter	K	David City, - Neb.
Samuel Russell	K	Metz, Jasper Co.. Iowa.
Eli Williams	K	Floyd P. O., - Penn'a.
John Bergwin	L	Rockland P. O., "
D. S. Smith	L	Rockland " "
John S. Roberts	L	Rockland " "
John Huston	L	Franklin, - "
S. W. Pryor	L	Cranberry P. O., "
S. Bergwin	L	Turkey City, "
Ed. Bergwin	L	Coal City, - "
Henry Neely	L	Rockland P. O., "
Liberty Estis	L	Lake Pleasant, "
E. C. Spencer	L	West Liberty, Penn,a.
Jno. Montgomery	L	Nickleville, - "
John Hagan	L	Brooklyn, - N. Y.
C. H. W. Ruhe	L	Pittsburgh, - Penn'a.

NAME.	COMPANY.	POST OFFICE.	
J. E. Estis	L	Lake Pleasant, Penn'a.	
Daniel Brown	L	Union City, -	"
Geo. Behers	L	Pittsburgh, -	"
John Donaldson	L	Pittsburgh, -	"
Thomas Parker	L	Pittsburgh, -	"
Robt. Fowler	L	Pittsburgh, -	"
Martin Geering	M	Geering, -	Neb.
L. H. Conrad	M	Carbondale, -	Penn'a.
John Ulmer	M	Carbondale, -	"
G. M. Felton	M	South Gibson,	"
Bradner Mapes	M	Clifford P. O.,	"
D. R. Stouffer	M	Mt. Pleasant,	"
Elias J. Harding	M	Pickville, -	"
Al. Brenneman	M	Freeport,	"
John Sweeney	M	Freeport, -	"
A. W. Robertson		Cooperstown,	"
J. S. Davison		Sunville P. O.,	"
Ethan Stone		Franklin, -	"
Cyrus R. Dennison		Sunville P. O.,	"
August Epert		Franklin, -	"
James C. Morrison		Franklin, -	"
James Wilson		West Green,	"
W. E. Gray		Franklin, -	"
John Jones		Franklin, -	"

HONORARY MEMBERS.

James B. Clew	Pittsburgh, -	Penn'a.	
John H. Covode	Grand Rapids,	Mich.	
Wm. Collingwood	Pittsburgh, -	Penn'a.	
J. Morton Hall	Pittsburgh, -	"	
E. M. Biddle	Pittsburgh, -	"	
Mrs. Jane Welton	Franklin, -	"	
Marshall Kerr	Kerrtown, -	"	
Capt. John A. Wiley	Franklin, -	"	
T. H. Childs	Pittsburgh, -	"	
H. Childs	Pittsburgh, -	"	
A. H. Childs	Pittsburgh, -	"	

58

CONTRIBUTIONS TO MONUMENT.

NAME.	COMPANY.	AMOUNT.
Capt. A. M. Beatty		$ 5 00
S. Burgwin		5 00
Maj. D. C. Phillips		100 00
Gen. W. E. Doster		100 00
Maj. John C. Paul		100 00
Jno. H. Covode, Hon. Member		25 00
Capt. W. K. Gillespie	E	25 00
John T. Ewens	I	10 00
Dr. C. P. Seip	B	10 00
John Boyce	B	10 00
A. H. & H. Childs, Hon. Members		50 00
Wm. H. Collingwood	E	25 00
W. Collingwood, Hon. Member		10 00
Dr. J. J. Green	C	10 00
T. H. Childs, Honorary Member		50 00
G. H. Tiel	E	10 00
John Irvin	B	1 00
Ewens & Eberle		10 00
Capt. A. A. Plumer	I	50 00
Venango Bat. Ass'n, 4th Pa. Cav.		50 00
Maj. J. B. Maitland	L	25 00
Capt. J. R. Grant	K	25 00
B. F. Crain	I	5 00
W. H. Collingwood	E	5 00
Capt. Alex. Frazier	I	5 00
W. H. Cramer	K	2 00
Capt. J. M. Gayetty	H	2 00
W. H. Varner	H	1 00
A. J. Pryor	L	1 00
W. G. Sheppard	L	1 00
I. H. Morgan		1 00
W. C. Bigler	K	1 00
C. James	I	1 00
J. R. Downing	H	1 00
H. M. Black	K	1 00
Robert S. Sarver	K	1 00
S. R. Weston	K	1 00

59

LIST OF CONTRIBUTORS

TO MONUMENTAL FUND AND EXPENSE OF REUNION, AT GETTYSBURG, PA., SEPTEMBER 11TH, 1889.

NAME.	COMP.	POST-OFFICE.		AMOUNT.
Gen. W. E. Doster	A	Bethlehem,	- Penn'a.	$10 00
Maj. R. J. Phipps	H	Clintonville,	- "	11 00
A. T. Felton	M	Carbondale,	- "	1 00
J. B. Woodling	K	Jackson Centre,	"	1 00
Geo. W. Crawford	B	Dixmont,	- "	1 00
J. H. Leasher	C	Pleasant Unity,	"	1 00
W. J. Boyd	A	Mauch Chunk,	"	1 00
Samuel M. West	C	Apollo,	- "	1 00
Jas. Caldwell	D	Brinton,	- "	2 00
Dr. W. B. Price		Berlin,	- Illinois,	5 00
Jas. Ogden	D	Latrobe,	- Penn'a.'	5 00
L. S. Cline	E	Leechburg	- "	1 00
Jas. A. Van Horn	B	Hunlock's Creek,	"	2 00
H. M. Kerr	E	Boston,	- "	1 00
C. C. Kirchner	C	Latrobe,	- "	1 00
Jas. Patton	E	Elizabeth,	- "	2 00
Wm. Steiner	A	Mauch Chunk,	- "	2 00
Lieut. Jas. A. Morrison	E	Branchton,	- "	2 00
Chas. O. Ellis	M	Waymart,	- "	5 00
L. J. Adams	M	Carbondale,	- "	1 00
David Cupps	E	Butler,	- - "	1 00
Hugh Crawford	B	Canton,	- - "	2 00
Geo. Schlager	A	Scranton,	- "	1 00
Capt. Alfred Darte, Jr.	M	Wilkes-Barre,	- "	25 00
D. R. P. Gates	K	Elk City,	- "	50
L. C. Darte	M	Wilkes-Barre,	- "	10 00
J. B. Gailey	L	Seneca,	- - "	5 00
R. P. Clark	H	Lottsville,	- "	50
Daniel Keester	K	Franklin,	- "	1 00
Thos. M. Dias	E	Elizabeth,	- "	1 00
J. Vandermark	M	Carbondale,	- "	5 00
J. L. Stouffer	C	Greensburg,	- "	50
J. N. Hoskinson	D	Bolivar,	- "	1 00

NAME.	COMP.	POST-OFFICE.		AMOUNT.
H. Bender...	I	Wallaceville, -	Penn'a.	1 00
W. H. Devenney.......	I	Franklin, -	"	1 00
Geo. Ghearing..........	I	Dempseytown,	"	1 00
Dr. J. J. Green..........	C	Pittsburgh, -	"	3 00
Fred. Berge	M	Scranton, -	"	1 00
Maj D. C. Phillips......	F	Pittsburg, -	"	10 00
Jas. Painter..........	E	Manor Station,	"	2 00
Geo. A. Dewoody	H	Balliet, - -	"	50
R. B. Fraser..........	A	Pittsburgh, -	"	2 00
A. T. Malin...........	C	Robbins, - -	"	1 00
Thos. Lockwood........	E	Greenoch, -	"	50
John Lamb............	E	Boston, - -	"	2 00
W. H. Vantassel	C	Appollo, - -	"	1 00
Jno. G. Robinson......	D	West Fairfield, -	"	1 00
Isaac J. Robb.........	D	New Florence, -	"	1 00
James R. Knox....	D	Manhattan, Riley Co., Kan.		5 00
Jos. Moreland.........	B	New Wilmington, Penn'a.		1 00
John B. Yost....	A	Hazelton, -	"	1 00
J. Lichtenfelt....	D	Bolivar, - -	"	1 00
John Quinn	G	Pittsburgh, -	"	1 00
Geo. Brown...........	B	Economy, -	"	1 00
Condy Gallagher.......	A	Lansford, -	"	1 00
Jos. McLaughlin........	A	Summit Hill, -	"	1 00
C. S. Mark	I	Franklin, -	"	1 00
J. M. Bethune.........	I	Knox, - -	"	2 00
R. P. Seely...........	I	Wallaceville, -	"	1 00
Lee Wilson...........	B	Murdocksville,	"	1 00
Wm. Cruikshank	B	Verona, - -	"	1 00
Alex. Campsie........	A	East Mauch Chunk,	"	35
Samuel Heath	E	Boston, - -	"	10
John H. Ulrich........	F	Annville, - -	"	1 00
R. H. Keiffer	F	" - -	"	25
G. K. Hess............	F	Lebanon, - -	"	1 00
S. Wise............ ...	K	Franklin, -	"	1 00
Lieut. Geo. W. Wise....	K	Callensburg, -	"	1 00
D. L. Miller.... ...	H	Franklin, -	"	50
John Barber..........	C	Paulton, - -	"	2 00
S. C. Bole	E	Leechburg, -	"	2 00

NAME.	COMP.	POST-OFFICE.		AMOUNT.
T. J. Edwards	A	Mahanoy City,	Penn'a.	1 50
A. R. Sloan	K	Eldred, - -	"	3 00
W. J. Stewart	G	Sewickley, -	"	1 00
David Ray	H	Cooperstown, -	"	1 00
T. T. Watt	I	Wallaceville, -	"	1 00
Cal. James	I	Oil City, -	"	1 00
Benj. Cabel	D	Bolivar, - -	"	50
J. S. Duncan	C	East Sandy, -	"	50
T. C. Byrnes	I	Cranberry, -	"	1 00
John Sweeney	M	Freeport, -	"	50
G. W. Conrad	M	Glenwood; -	"	1 00
S. Stouffer	C	Greensburg, -	"	1 00
Dr. W. G. Bishop	L	Brookville, -	"	2 00
Levi Porter	K	Clintonville, -	"	2 00
John W. Moore	G	Pittsburgh, -	"	5 00
Capt. A. M. Beatty	H	Dempseytown,	"	2 00
Capt. Wm. Hyndman	A	Ketcham, -	Idaho,	50 00

Paid Expenses of Reunion.......... ....$71 15

62

VENANGO BATTALION ASSOCIATION.

COMPANIES H, I, K AND L.

On January 16, 1887, the following members met at Franklin, Pa.: J. R. Grant, A. M. Beatty, Alex. Frazier, C. S. Mark, L. D. Davis and John Huston, for the purpose of arranging for a reunion of the battalion. Letters from comrades were read, concurring in the object. After effecting an oganization, adjourned to meet on the 19th of January. John P. Barr was appointed historian, with request to prepare a paper to be read at the coming reunion. Additional names were added to the committee, and adjourned to meet January 21st. Committee of Arrangements met as per adjournment, and fixed on April 8th for the reunion, and the proper steps taken to carry out the plan.

REUNION OF VENANGO BATTALION,

APRIL 8TH, 1887.

The first reunion of the Venango Battalion of the Fourth Pennsylvania Cavalry was held in Franklin, April 8th, 1887, at 2 o'clock, P. M. Captain J. R. Grant called the comrades to attention, and in his introductory remarks said the committee of arrangements had sent out letters of invitation to the boys and thought a great fraud had been perpetrated, as he saw before him a lot of gray headed men, but, if properly vouched for, the proceedings would begin. They were identified accordingly, and the first meeting was opened by a hearty welcome from the Mayor in behalf of the city. R. H. Woodburn, of W. B. Mays Post, No. 220, cordially extended a welcome and the hospitality of the Post during the stay in the city, and right royally it was carried out, the citizens vieing with each other to do honor to the veterans. A committee of five was appointed on permanent organization, consisting of

63

J. B. Maitland, Chas. E. Taylor, A. M. Beatty, Alex. Frazier and Levi Porter, who, through their chairman, reported the following, which was adopted: President, Cyrus S. Mark; Vice-Presidents, A. M. Beatty, Co. H; R. W. Shaw, Co. K; A. J. Pryor, Co. L; Secretary, John Huston; Corresponding Secretary, L. D. Davis; Treasurer, J. R. Grant; Historian, J. B. Maitland; Chaplain, Rev. B. F. Crane.

On motion it was decided to hold the second reunion in Franklin, on the first Friday in April, 1888. Adjourned to meet at 7 o'clock, P. M., in the Court House. The order to "fall in" was given, and the line of march taken to the Exchange Hotel, where the banquet was served in its own superb style. The boys, with their usual impetuosity, succeeded in getting the better of even a very large supply of edibles. Returning to the Court House, Judge C. E. Taylor, of Co. I, gave one of his happy addresses and prepared all for the good cheer of the evening. Porter Phipps, of the Sixteenth Pennsylvania Cavalry, did honor to the Fourth when he stated that General Gregg selected nearly every member of his staff from the Fourth, and five of them from the Venango Battalion. Maj. McClintock, of Oil City, offered the following resolution: "We, the survivors of the Fourth Regiment Pennsylvania Cavalry, having extended our session to the morning of April 9th, in commemoration of the surrender of Gen. Lee, at Appomattox, do, in this twenty-second anniversary of that momentous event, drop a tear on the graves of our dead comrades of the long ago, and congratulate the living upon the magnificent results of the successful close of the war for the Union, and the almost miraculous realization of our fondest hopes and aspirations, and send greeting to all comrades of the old Pennsylvania Brigade, and extend a cordial invitation to meet with us at our next reunion."

The Court House was tastefully decorated, and among the pictures hung about the room was an oil painting of Col. J. H. Childs, who fell at Antietam, Sept. 17th, 1862. It is not saying too much that never was commander idolized as was Col. Childs, and the men were much moved at the sight of him, who always had a kind greeting for his men.

64

SECOND REUNION OF VENANGO BATTALION,

HELD AT FRANKLIN, PA., APRIL 1ST, 1888.

President C. S. Marks called attention; the divine bless-
ing invoked by Chaplain Crane, and the second reunion was
open for business. Minutes read and approved. The President gave a brief history of the Association, its objects and
aims. R. W. Dunn, President of Select Council, in the absence
of Mayor Lewis, welcomed the members in well-chosen words.
A committee on place of holding next reunion, selected Oil
City, and the time, April 26, 1889. Election of officers
resulted as follows: President, J. B. Maitland; First Vice-
President, A. A. Plumer; Second Vice-President, Wm. C.
Bigler; Third Vice-President, Geo. Ganing; Recording Secretary, J. M. Gayetty; Corresponding Secretary, Calvin James;
Treasurer, J. B. Maitland; Chaplain, Franklin Flowers.

Resolution: That a Publishing Committee of five members be appointed, to whom all matters pertaining to the publication of a history of the regiment, or the battalion, shall be
referred. The question of the erection of a monument at
Gettysburg was then considered. The plans and specifications
submitted, proposing a height of 10 feet, width of 7 feet, thick-
ness of 2 feet, weight of 38,440 lbs.; estimated cost $2,100.00.
Subscriptions to the fund asked for and a hearty response.

A. M. Beatty read a letter from the War Department, Adj't
General's office, saying: "In reply to your inquiry, I have the
honor to inform you that so far as shown by the records on
file in this office, the Fourth Pennsylvania Cavalry was
engaged in at least 75 combats of various degrees of magni-
tude. There is also indirect evidence that the regiment as a
whole or in part, participated in other affairs, but the defective
character of the regimental records makes a full and complete
record of them impracticable." (Signed O. D. Green, Ass't
Ad'j-Gen'l.)

65

A list of battles in which the regiment had participated was then given, numbering 77 in all. Adjournment to supper at 4:30 P. M., the line formed, but was confronted by a photographer, and a picture of the Venango Battalion was the result of the affray. The United States and Exchange Hotels supplied all our wants in a fine banquet, provided by the city.

Before the camp was ablaze, in the matter of a history it was left to the Historian to appoint a member from each of the four companies composing the battalion. An escort, W. B. Mays Post, headed by the Franklin Cornet Band, preceded us to the Opera House, which was crowded to its utmost. The stage was a representation of the camp, and brought back scenes of "Auld Lang Syne." Comrade Boyer gave a lucid description of camp-life,—its joys and its sorrows. Maj. McClintock regaled the audience with anecdotes of army life. J. R. Grant recalled the fact, that just twenty-three years ago that night, the Fourth Cavalry was at Sailor's Creek, Va. That day they captured 6,000 prisoners, including 20 women on their way from Richmond, and enough artillery and supply wagons to fill a five acre field. He gave a graphic account of the scenes through which the regiment passed from the 2nd to the 9th of April, 1865, when the Appomattox surrender took place. It was a fact, he said, that the Fourth Cavalry closed the fight at Appomattox. In concluding, he did not wish to be understood as claiming that the Fourth Cavalry did all the fighting in the war. The rest of the army rendered much assistance; in fact, the Fourth Cavalry were nobly supported by the Army of the Potomac all the way through. [Laughter.]

Addresses by Porter Phipps, of the Sixteenth Pennsylvania Cavalry, A. M. Beatty, A. G. Wilkins, (alias "Corporal Schnapps,") together with the fine music discoursed by the quartette led by Prof. Kinsley, enlivened the evening, making all feel that is was good to be there. The attendance was nearly one hundred.

It is proposed to hold the next reunion at Butler, Pa., on the same date that the regiment meets, when all business matters can be arranged and a time for holding the next battalion reunion determined.

66

FOURTH REUNION.

A committee of arrangements was appointed by Col. W. E. Doster, President of the Association, August 11th, 1890. consisting of Dr. C. P. Seip, Dr. J. J. Green, W. H. Collingwood, John T. Ewens, John Boyce, R. B. Fraser, John W. Moore and Wm. K. Gillespie.

Several meetings were held and arrangements made to hold our Fourth Reunion on October 1st, 1890. The programme was for a business meeting at Veteran Legion Hall. Sixth Avenue, at 2 P. M.; banquet at Seventh Avenue Hotel. at 8 P. M. The regiment assembled at the Seventh Avenue Hotel on the morning of October 1st; Mr. Wilson, the proprietor, having generously placed three parlors at the service of the members as reception rooms. A most delightful morning was passed in meetings, greetings and reminiscences, and at 1:30 P. M., the Regiment formed, about 130 present, and escorted by a drum corps, marched to the Veteran Legion Hall, Sixth Avenue. The meeting was called to order by Dr. C. P. Seip, Chairman of Executive Committee, and lead in prayer by Chaplain H. Q. Graham. Dr. Seip then introduced Major J. B. Maitland, Vice-President of the Association, as presiding officer. Major Maitland, on account of the absence of minutes of the Gettysburg meeting in 1889, gave a sketch of the organization effected at Gettysburg, September 12th. 1889, he stated that since then, the Regimental Monument had been completed. inspected by the building committee, and accepted October 29th, 1889; and that the monument is a marvel of beauty. and will delight every member of the regiment. when they shall have the pleasure of seeing it.

Minutes of Capt. Darte, Recording Secretary, of business meeting at Gettysburg, September 12th, 1889, were then read. also action of that meeting completing the permanent organization as follows: President, W. E. Doster; Vice-President. J. B. Maitland; Corresponding Secretary, W. H. Collingwood; Recording Secretary, Wm. K. Gillespie; Treasurer. J. R. Grant.

67

The Constitution and By-Laws adopted at reunion in Pittsburgh, in 1875, were then read and adopted, as the Constitution and By-Laws of this organization.

On motion of Comrade Collingwood, it was unanimously-agreed to change the Constitution as to permanent officers, so as to provide for the office of Chaplain.

Letters of acceptance and regret were then read by the Secretary, some of them conveying the mournful tidings of the death of comrades, and bearing words of love and affection from surviving relatives of the following comrades: John Anderson, Co. K; Daniel McKee, Co. H; H. A. Ross, Co. I; Parcus Copeland, Co. H. Others from comrades, who would, but could not come, and all bearing messages of good will and expressing the intensity of affection lodged in the hearts of comrades of the old Fourth, for each other.

President Maitland then made a statement regarding the battle of Stony Creek, stating that the credit of that success was claimed by the Sixteenth Pennsylvania Cavalry. He stated clearly, facts showing that the Fourth captured the Fort, and about 200 prisoners,—a larger number than were present of the Fourth—burned a great quantity of stores, together with storage houses, and returned inside of 20 minutes, when just then Hampton's Rebels came in sight, but they were compelled to accept the situation and bottle their wrath.

The President also read, from his Diary, as follows:

STONY CREEK.

FROM DIARY OF MAJ. J. B. MAITLAND.

December 1, 1864—Thursday.—Precisely at 3:30 A. M., were in the saddle, and moved on the Lee's Mill road in the following order: Thirteenth Pennsylvania, Fourth Pennsylvania, section Second Pennsylvania, section Sixteenth Pennsylvania, Eighth Pennsylvania, The advance found the mill and bridge burned at Lee's Mill, and the column was delayed till daylight. Thence struck the plank road at Proctor's, and moved from there southward to Rowanty Creek, where a picket was found and quickly dislodged; pushed across and to the Railroad; found that a train had just left. At Stony

68

Creek the rebels fired several signal guns, calling, no doubt, for help. We moved down on a charge to Stony Creek Station, dismounted the Sixteenth Pennsylvania, and threw the Fourth Pennsylvania, mounted, well on the left of the works. It charged and also the dismounted men, and in 20 minutes 3 guns were ours, the works, and 200 prisoners, and an immense lot of stores, which, together with buildings, cars, etc., were fired and destroyed. Returned to camp at 9 P. M., having accomplished a march of 50 miles. The Thirteenth and Second Pennsylvania were left on picket.

CASUALTIES:—OFFICERS.

Lieut. Luther Day, Co. K, 16th Penn'a, killed.
Lieut. Chas. White, Co. I, 13th   "   wounded.
Lieut. O'Callaghan, Co. E,   "   "   "
Capt. Ervay,   Co. I, 4th   "   "

ENLISTED MEN.

REG'T.	KILLED.	WOUNDED.	MISSING.
2d Penn'a	0	0	0
4th "	2	12	1
8th "	0	0	0
13th "	0	0	0
16th "	0	9	0

President Maitland also filed the following bearing on and confirming the claim of the Fourth for that action:

STONY CREEK.

"TOBIE." HISTORY OF THE FIRST MAINE.

"Reveille at 2 o'clock in the morning of Dec. 1st, 1864. Our dream of rest in camp vanished, and cross and sleepy, the command marched via McCann's, Lee's Mills and the Jerusalem Plank Road for Stony Creek Station, the point on the Weldon Railroad from which the rebels wagoned their supplies around the left of the army. The rebel pickets were found at Rowanty Creek. The brigade pressed rapidly forward to Stony Creek Station, some two miles from the Rowanty bridge, and reached there early in the day. The

enemy's works consisted of two small forts, with several pieces of artillery in position on the south side of Stony Creek and both sides of the railroad, with lines of works extending on the flanks of the forts. Gen. Gregg ordered the Fourth to cross the creek below the fortifications without delay, and attack the rebels in the rear. It did so in most gallant style, under a heavy fire from the enemy, who had a perfect range of the ford. Halting a moment to reform, the regiment charged under command of Maj. W. B. Mays, in rear of the railroad, and then directly down to the railroad to and between the forts, where they dismounted and actually charged, with pistol and saber in hand, over the works, forcing the enemy to surrender unconditionally and at once. The regiment captured more men than it numbered, burned all the rebel stores, which were numerous, the station and the high bridge over Stony Creek, and in twenty minutes time returned with the prisoners. Hampton's headquarters were only four miles from the station, and the dashing engagement took place almost in the suburbs of his camp, and haste was necessary, for on the heels of the "boys in blue," came Hampton, who was obliged to bottle his anger a while longer, as the battery of the Third Brigade poured canister through their columns. The First Maine destroyed the bridge across Rowanty. The regiment reached camp at midnight, and the rebel taunt of " beef" henceforth was answered by "Stony Creek."

STONY CREEK.—BATES' HISTORY.

"At Stony Creek, Dec. 1, 1864, Gregg's cavalry and a battery were engaged, in which the Fourth performed gallant service. It was led by Maj. Mays. A fort near the point where the railroad crosses the run, stood in the way of further advance, and it was necessary to capture it. This duty was assigned to the Fourth. Plunging into the stream, it crossed above, and making a detour, came in upon and attacked the rear of the work, while the front facing the river was held by the Sixteenth Cavalry, dismounted. Assailed thus in front and rear, the garrison was soon compelled to surrender. Two

hundred prisoners, three cannon, with arms, equipments and stores, were captured. The loss was considerable. Capt. Francis M. Ervay was among the wounded."

The following correspondence was afterwards furnished by the President for incorporation in the minutes, as contributing to establish our claim:

OIL CITY, October 26, 1890.

MR. F. D. GARMAN, Mifflingtown, Pa.:

DEAR SIR AND COMRADE:—I was very much interested in the history of the Sixteenth Cavalry, read at the reunion at Franklin, on the 24th inst., especially in that referring to the action at Stony Creek, in which I think your claims too strong, as well as the language imputing an attempt on the part of another regiment to steal your honors. I hope that sentence will be expunged from your forthcoming history, and that you will allow the credit due the Fourth Pennsylvania Cavalry, who, with the Sixteenth Pennsylvania Cavalry, jointly achieved a splendid victory. The casualties in the Fourth denote sufficiently clear the part borne by that regiment.

Yours in F., C. & L.,

J. B. MAITLAND.

MIFFLINTOWN, October 1, 1890.

MAJOR J. B MAITLAND, Oil City:

DEAR SIR AND COMRADE:—The intention of my story of the regiment was neither to give the record of another regiment, nor to reflect on it, but simply to give ours. As you will recollect, our regiment charged dismounted, and crossed the creek on the railroad bridge, stepping from tie to tie. This, too, in front of the fort. The smallness of our loss was due to the fact that a large gun, trained to sweep the bridge, could not be fired because of the fact that the charge, as it was being rammed home, stuck, and before this could be remedied our boys were upon them. All you say about the "Gallant Fourth" is true, and I join in any encomiums you give them. They were to the left, and of course our efforts without them, as theirs without us, would have been futile.

71

There have been efforts made to take from us not only what we did at Stony Creek, but also at Trevilian Station and St. Mary's Church, but not by yourself or the Fourth Pennsylvania Cavalry Association, for whom "our boys," as well as myself, retain the kindest remembrance.

Yours Fraternally,   F. D. GARMAN.

HEADQUARTERS 2D BRIGADE, 2D DIV.,
   CAVALRY CORPS, ARMY OF THE POTOMAC,
     BEFORE PETERSBURG, VA., DEC. 3, 1864.

GENERAL ORDERS)
   No. 16.   )

The Colonel commanding takes this opportunity to congratulate and compliment the officers and men of the Second Brigade, on their conduct in the brilliant affair at Stony Creek Station. The rapidity of your advance, and the impetuosity of your attack, called forth remarks of approbation from all who witnessed your assault upon the enemy's works, and places the capture of Stony Creek Station amongst the most brilliant achievements of the war. You have demonstrated to the world your ability to successfully assault well constructed earth works—with artillery in position and fully manned—even when situated between a deep and wide creek. Your previous history has won for you the name of the "Fighting Brigade." Stony Creek will add to that, the name of the "Dashing Brigade."

(Signed)   J. IRVIN GREGG,
Col. and B't Brig. Gen. Comdg. Brigade.

JOHN B. YOST writes:—"Stony Creek Station was my last fight in the war. Was wounded in the right shoulder in that engagement and went to Lincoln Hospital, and was discharged May 12, 1865." He justly claims for the regiment the honor of being the only mounted body that charged a fort, and for himself the distinguished honor of being the first man to reach the works, although wounded when about forty yards from them, and his horse killed at the fort. The gallantry of the men in that charge was conspicuous. (See "Tobie," and notes from the diary of the A. A. G.)

72

The President also furnished from his Diary the record of the votes of the Fourth for President of the United States in 1864:

COMPANY.	McCLELLAN.	LINCOLN.
A	26	12
B	2	29
C	8	18
D	5	24
E	1	30
F	9	20
G	7	43
H	19	8
I	8	24
K	6	28
L	4	31
M	12	8
Total	107	275

Corresponding Secretary Collingwood called attention to inaccuracies in Bates' History, and stated that many casualties were not reported, and that many comrades, who had served long terms in the regiment, were not recorded, and suggested that company organizations be formed for the purpose of completing company and individual records, and compiling and recording facts for regimental history.

Comrade Hon. M. A. Foran, Co. E, now of Cleveland, O., was called on and made a very interesting address, with reminiscences of our last campaign in the Spring of 1865 up to Appomattox.

President Maitland read blank forms with notice that copies would be sent to comrades asking for personal information as to facts and experiences, for use in preparing regimental history, and urged each survivor to fill the blanks and mail them to the Historian.

Comrade Edwards being called for sang a song, " Let Me Like a Soldier Fall."

Rev. Turner, son of the first Chaplain of the Regiment, was introduced, and in a short address told of his being, when

a very small boy, with the regiment in Camp Sprague, Washington, D. C. in 1862, and of the return in poor health, and the death of his father in 1864.

Capt. Beatty furnished a complete record of the names of Co. H. Capt. Boggs, who came from the far west, 1500 miles, to attend the reunion, suggested that in consideration of his long march, the haversack and canteen furnished by the Commissary should be well filled and contain what any Commissary of the Fourth should know would be a requisite after a long march. President Maitland called attention to the faithful and efficient work done by Comrade Collingwood, and the Association gave him a most hearty vote of thanks. Collingwood being called for, made one of his most effective speeches to prove that the Association was being taken in, and that he hadn't done much.

Comrade Robert Painter introduced his aged mother, who gave three sons to Co. E, all good soldiers and faithful to the end. She was greeted by the Association and invited to attend the banquet.

The election of officers was then proceeded with, resulting as follows : President, J. B. Maitland ; Vice-President, Thos. J. Edwards ; Chaplain, H. Q. Graham ; Corresponding Secretary, W. H. Collingwood ; Recording Secretary, Wm. K. Gillespie ; Treasurer, J. R. Grant ; Executive Committee, B. M. Duncan, Co. G ; David Cupps, Co. E. ; A. M. Borland, Co. G. ; Geo. D. McFarland, Co. G. ; Auditing Committee, R. J. Phipps, David Cupps.

Suggestions for place of next reunion, including Philadelphia, Greensburg, Leechburg and Butler were made and Butler was decided upon by a large majority.

Comrade Cupps pledged Butler for a hearty reception and entertainment, and offered a resolution thanking the committee of arrangements for the manner of conducting their work, preparatory to the reunion. Thos. J. Edwards offered remarks and resolution advocating the interest of the members in the commutation of Capt. G. W. Moss' death sentence. President Maitland sketched his soldier life, Collingwood

reported many of his acts of bravery, and said that his record was without one unfavorable trait. Comrade Cupps offered the following:

Resolved, That a committee of five, familiar with the life and services of Capt. G. W. Moss, be appointed to represent this Association, in doing all that can be done to secure the commutation of sentence of our comrade.

The committee appointed was as follows: Chairman, A. M. Beatty, R. J. Phipps, J. B. Maitland and M. A. Foran.

Comrade Edwards sang a song, and Chaplain Graham pronounced the benediction, and the Association adjourned to meet at the banquet hall at 8 P. M.

BANQUET.

About 8:15 P. M., the veterans, with their wives, fell in line, and keeping step to the sound of the sweet music furnished by the Cathedral Band, they were ushered into the large banquet hall, where an elaborate supper had been prepared by the host, Mr. B. C. Wilson. After all had taken seats at the various tables, a prayer was offered by the Chaplain, Rev. H. Q. Graham.

DR. C. P. SEIP arose and said:—

COMRADES, LADIES AND GENTLEMEN:—We have with us to-night nearly every comrade whose address we could find to meet with us to partake of this banquet. Among others, we have invited a few of the infantry and artillery forces, without whom our organization was never perfect. It was our pleasure frequently to open an engagement in order to get the infantry and artillery to fight. We have them with us to-night, and they will fight their battles here as they did in olden times. I now introduce to you our Toast Master, Major J. B. Maitland.

MAJOR MAITLAND, who was greeted with applause, said:—

COMRADES, LADIES AND GENTLEMEN:—The Fourth Pennsylvania Cavalry never claimed to have secured the great victory and peace achieved alone. It was in connection with the other arms of the service, and therefore, we are very glad to meet those to-night who represent these other arms of the

service. We promise you now a rare treat furnished by our host; and later on, at the last of the feast, we will have, we trust, the best of the wine.

While beautiful strains of music floated through the banquet hall, the veterans and their guests partook of the following elegantly prepared

MENU.

BLUE POINTS.

CONSOMME PRINTANIERE.

CALIFORNIA SALMON, STEAMED, SAUCE HOLLANDAISE.

POTATOES, A LA JULIENNE.

SLICED TOMATOES.   QUEEN OLIVES.   CELERY.

FROZEN SHERBET, AU CHARTREUSE.

SPRING CHICKEN BROILED, A LA MAITRE D' HOTEL.

ASPARAGUS, WITH DRESSING.

SWEETBREAD IN CASE.   FRENCH PEAS.

DEVILED CRABS, BALTIMORE STYLE.   SWEET POTATOES, FRIED.

CHICKEN SALAD.   SHRIMP SALAD.

TUTTI FRUTTI ICE CREAM.   ORNAMENTED CAKE.   ASSORTED CAKES.   FRUIT.

DEIDSHEIMER WINE JELLY.   CONFECTIONERY.   PINEAPPLE CHEESE.

CRACKERS.   TEA AND COFFEE.

At the close of this delightful feast, Comrade T. J. Edwards, Co. A, was introduced, who favored the audience with a medley which was received with hearty applause.

MAJOR MAITLAND: We have with us to-night one whom it is not necessary for me to introduce to you, for his name is well known to all of us—our guest, Gen. A. L. Pearson. After the applause had subsided,

GEN. PEARSON said:—

MR. CHAIRMAN, LADIES AND GENTLEMEN:—Many years ago I had the pleasure of forming the acquaintance of very many members of the Fourth Pennsylvania Cavalry, because we were thieves together, or very nearly so. I am here to acknowledge that I was at that time the receiver of stolen goods. Even to-night, as I came into the banquet hall, Comrade Frazier, who is sitting in the near neighborhood, remarked to me, "I think the last horse you got was a stolen sorrel that I gave you." He is a little mistaken as to that being the last

horse I got from the Fourth Pennsylvania Cavalry. The last one I got was a miserable affair. An hour or two before the battle of Preble's Farm, I had the misfortune to have a very valuable animal shot, and, as usual, I sent a note over to ˜Col. Young of the Fourth to loan me a horse. He did. It was shortly afterwards shot, and I sent a second note to the worthy gentleman, and he sent me a three-year old black colt that had never been shod, and never had a bridle bit in his mouth. I had to have a horse ; it was necessary at that time ; so I mounted and did the best I could. I think Young intended that which came very near happening, namely, to get me into the hands of the enemy. I wanted the horse to go one way, he wanted to go the other. I am sorry to say he wanted to go toward the enemy, and I didn't. [Laughter.] That was bad enough ; but two or three years ago I heard from Col. Young in Texas. He had the impertinence to send me an itemized bill, in which he charged for every horse that he had ever loaned me, and expected payment. Well, I knew very well that he hadn't bought the horses, because the Fourth Pennsylvania Cavalry never was noted for purchasing horses, [Laughter] and it was the best mounted cavalry regiment connected with the Army of the Potomac. I paid for the horses —I sent him a three-cent postage stamp, and got a one-cent stamp in return. Young and I are at least square to-day. I have very many pleasant recolections of the Fourth Pennsylvania Cavalry. I remember very distinctly when they were out with the Fifth Corps on a little reconnoisance toward, I think Lynchburg.

A voice: Apple-jack raid.

Gen. Pearson : I stand corrected ; it was the apple-jack raid. I remember that the cavalry was in front. I remember distinctly that we found the empty casks lying about when we got up. The Fourth Pennsylvania Cavalry, as usual, had been there ahead of us ; and there were the casks, marked "Apple Jack," but "Jack" was gone. [Laughter.]

I remember upon that occasion, just at noon, there was a halt, and many of the Fourth Cavalry went out skirmishing — not for the enemy. Some came in ladened with geese ; a

number had pieces of boards upon their heads ladened with honey, and piled up in pyramidal shape. It was a rather warm day, and the honey ran down ; the bugle sounded, and they moved up near us with handfuls of feathers dropping off them. ' Well I don't know whether they looked like cavalry or geese ; [Laughter] but they had the honey and goose too.

I remember distinctly a few things that were not so bright and pleasant. I remember the Fifth Corps standing under arms when you men fought at Ream's Station. I remember leaving my command and going towards Ream's Station and getting there just about the heat of the battle when one of your officers, Frank Parke, received the wound that afterwards killed him. I remember that terrible conflict. I remember the action of the Fourth Cavalry, and I remember many actions in which they were engaged, a number of which I saw myself; and I say to-night, as I have said many, many hundreds of times before, that no better men ever mounted the back of a horse ; no better men ever drew the sabre in battle ; no better men did more to sustain the grand old Government and keep the old flag afloat, than you men here to-night, and the dead comrades that have gone ; and I hope and pray that this, your fourth annual reunion, will be but one of very many ; and I hope and pray that when next you meet the man that stands to-day acknowledged as one of the finest cavalry officers in the regular army, Col. S. B. M. Young, will be with you. [Applause.]

MAJOR MAITLAND :—Comrade Seip will now read a letter from our Comrade S. B. M. Young.

COMRADE SEIP:—This letter was just received this evening, and reads as follows :

SEPTEMBER 25th, 1890.

MY DEAR DOCTOR :

I regret that I cannot be with the veterans of my old regiment, but you know that I always obeyed orders when in the field with you, and I have never forgotten that the first duty of a soldier is to obey. My orders here are of such a character that I am compelled to remain in the city with the command, but I assure you that in spirit I will be

with the old boys of the gallant Fourth Pennsylvania Cavalry.
May my old comrades who meet with you live long to fight
their battles over. Say to all of them that my prayers will be
with them. God bless them all.

Ever yours and their friend,

S. B. M. YOUNG.

COMRADE C. P. SEIP:—The reason why this letter came
too late to be read at the business meeting this afternoon was
from the fact that it was sent with another communication to
Gen. Pearson, and, as usual, he delayed handing it over. That
is characteristic of the man; he always keeps the best things
for the last. As to his story about the cavalry horses, I know
that he never gave you the remotest idea of the number of
horses that were procured for him by our regiment. Why, I
was detailed many a time to go out and steal a horse for the
General, [Laughter] and I venture to say there are many men
in the regiment to-day that stole more than one horse and
took it over to the 155th Pennsylvania. Gen. Pearson reported
many horses killed; how he killed them I don't know. The
colt he referred to, which Col. Young sent him last, was the
only effort we ever made that we thought would succeed in
getting him into a fight. [Laughter.] I am very glad he has
reformed since he came here. He doesn't steal any now
because he doesn't get a chance. Yet, he has told the truth;
we can all vouch for the fact that he did get into that fight,
and that his horse did go ahead, and it was on that occasion
that his regiment performed the most glorious deeds in its
whole career.

General Pearson:—I want to say—

Major Maitland:—General, the comrades are all busy with
Dr. Seip, and there will be no attention paid to anything else
said.

Gen. Pearson:—I can only say, Mr. Chairman, I know why
this is done. I have convicted them half a dozen times of
stealing hogs. [Laughter.]

Major Maitland:—These personalities, comrades, will not
be allowed in our own command; but as between men of different commands they are permitted.

79

Col. Gallupe was introduced, and greeted with applause. (Cries of " Heavy Artillery.")

COL. GALLUPE:—

I had the honor and pleasure of commanding all arms of the service, so that the heavy artillery is only a portion.

MR. PRESIDENT, LADIES AND GENTLEMEN:—I am not at all accustomed to addressing audiences of any kind, more especially an audience of this kind, and after the amusing and very interesting address of Gen. Pearson, for me to assume to say anything of a serious character would be decidedly out of place. Of course, I know a good deal of the history of your regiment—the Fourth Cavalry, it having been raised here and officered by a great many officers from this neighborhood, whom I met on many occasions, being connected with the Fifth Corps from its organization until the close of the war. The record of this regiment I had the honor and pleasure of placing on file in Washington City in 1869. I was detailed in the War Department for eleven months, and I wish to give you a little information, something you have probably never heard before, in regard to that matter. The cavalry regiments are all placed on file in one part of the War Department by themselves. The remarks of company officers and regimental officers are placed on each of the final muster-out rolls, and in going over these and making up the book in which a brief history of each regiment is entered, taken from the final muster-out rolls, there is but one regiment of cavalry I believe, in Pennsylvania, whose record is at all brighter than yours, if it is possible to be, and that is the First Pennsylvania Cavalry, or was originally the First Pennsylvania Cavalry. That regiment and your regiment stand pre-eminently among the first regiments of cavalry in the Army of the Potomac. That is a true record. The Harris Light Cavalry also has a remarkably good record; also, the Eighth Illinois Cavalry and the First New Jersey Cavalry. Those regiments stood very high; but your regiment and the First Pennsylvania Cavalry had the cleanest and best military record, I believe, if I remember aright, of any of the regiments of cavalry in the Army of the Potomac during the war.

80

I wish to say just one word in regard to one of your Colonels, who fell at the battle of Antietam. I was very well and intimately acquainted with him—Col. Childs. I had carried him an order, I think, about twenty minutes before he fell by the bridge—you gentlemen remember the place very well. An order had been sent on three different occasions by Gen. McClellan to Gen. Burnside to charge across the bridge. He made excuses, and gave three different and distinct reasons for not charging, and failed to do it, as you remember, until late in the afternoon. Had the charge been made when it was ordered first, Col. Childs would probably be alive to-day. It was on account of this delay that Col. Childs was there ; it was not intended that the cavalry should be there at that time, and on account of this delay Col. Childs happened to be in that particular locality. Hence, his death. He was a man who stood remarkably high in the estimation of his superior officers, and I am sure, in the estimation of all who ever met him or knew him.

Gentlemen, as I said before, I am not acustomed to making speeches and addresses, and I know that a speech to be at all interesting to old soldiers must be full of wit and humor. That is something I do not possess. Therefore, hoping that you will meet again and frequently, is the sincere wish of your humble servant. Good night.

MAJOR MAITLAND:—I can say we are very much gratified at the statements you have made to-night. We are striving at our reunions to make history for our regiment, and the statements you have given us to-night are new to us, and we are very much obliged.

Those who were at our business meeting this afternoon cannot doubt, if they ever did, the kindly feeling existing between soldiers, and especially between soldiers of the same regiment. Where all have done so well, it would be invidious to make any comparisons at all ; and yet, in our work as a regiment, beginning back fifteen years ago (our first regimental reunion being held in this city) we began then to make the history of our regiment. Many of our comrades have contributed largely to this end, but there is one among them

especially, who has given much time, and time that he could not well spare from his business. This regiment has twice taken occasion to honor that comrade; first, at Gettysburg, by a unanimous resolution of the comrades, thanking him for the arduous labors performed in connection with the erection of our monument; and again, for the pleasure of the present reunion we are largely indebted to this same comrade. He has taken time that really did not belong to him, time that should have been devoted to sleep, in order that he might further your interests and your pleasures at this reunion. There is no one, after what I have said, who will not fully understand whom I mean—Comrade W. H. Collingwood, [Applause) a man who has ever been true to the interests of the regiment. I will not say that I desire to cane him. We all love him too much for that; but, until very recently, we believed him, with one exception, to be the youngest member of the regiment. We have found out that he has been deceiving us somewhat, because another was reported to-day who joined us in 1865, who was only 15 years of age. But we forgive him, and will not withhold the cane on that account. Comrade Collingwood, I now have the pleasure on behalf of the Fourth Pennsylvania Cavalry, of bestowing upon you this their gift. [Applause.]

W. H. COLLINGWOOD:—

MR. PRESIDENT AND COMRADES:--This is a complete surprise to me, and I cannot express in fitting words my appreciation of your gift. So far as my work for the regiment is concerned, I would say that I simply did my duty, as best I could, as Corresponding Secretary; just as every member of the Fourth Cavalry has done his duty, if not more than his duty, heretofore. There is no organization with which I am connected, nor is there any person, from whom I appreciate a gift so much as from the regiment in which I served, from comrades whom I love, and with whom I stood side by side on the battle-field. The feeling with which soldiers who stood elbow to elbow in battle regard one another can not be imparted to, nor can it exist in those who were not in the

army. This gift, be assured, comrades, shall be cherished as long as I live. I thank you. [Applause.]

The cane is of ebony, handsomely mounted with gold, inscribed as follows:

W. H. COLLINGWOOD,
FROM HIS COMRADES OF THE
FOURTH PENNSYLVANIA CAVALRY,
OCTOBER 1, 1890.

Comrade Edwards, by special request, then sang "The Old Canteen."

MAJOR MAITLAND:

The word "Antietam" has peculiar significance to members of the Fourth Pennsylvania Cavalry. It has been referred to here to-night, and I am reminded of it as I look out upon the audience and see the wife of our old member, Capt. Hughes, and his son and daughter in the audience. I am reminded also, that on that day I was in command of the carbineers of Co. G, (I believe a Pittsburgh company), and when the word passed through the regiment that Col. Childs had fallen, it was almost impossible to hold those men to their posts of duty. Every man was ready to spring forward to the relief of Col. Childs. Our Comrade C. S. Mark will talk for a few moments on the subject of Antietam.

COMRADE MARK: —

LADIES AND GENTLEMEN, COMRADES:—I do not know that I have anything special to say, or of interest to the comrades, with reference to Antietam. You doubtless all remember the 17th day of September, 1862. If there is any one battle in which I had the honor to participate during my term of active service in the field that I remember distinctly, it is Antietam. I remember that early in the morning while we lay on the opposite side of the creek awaiting orders, all ready at a moment's notice to enter the engagement, the order finally came. You all remember with what haste the regiment crossed the Stone Bridge upon that morning. You also remember the regiment deploying to the left of the road and forming at the base of a hill upon the crest of which a battery was planted, and our purpose of forming there was to support

that battery. I remember that for at least an hour, if not more, it was a very warm place to be. The rebel batteries on the opposite hill had got in direct range of our battery, and they were sending the shot and shell in there pretty thick and fast. The range was so perfect, as you remember, their close, solid shot came, as it were, all to a certain point upon the crest of the him. Then all at once, it seemed they began to descend, passing right over the heads of the regiment so closely that we almost unconsciously, as we did on that occasion and often before, ducked our heads, and instantly got up again; and many was the remark made in reference to it. About that time, I remember a commotion throughout the ranks, and in few moments we learned its cause. Word was brought to us that Col. Childs had just fallen, mortally wounded. I think there was not a member of the regiment that did not feel at that moment the loss of Col. Childs. He was a manly officer, and a brave soldier. We felt keenly at the time our loss. We had another officer just at that time who had not had an opportunity hitherto of displaying much courage on the field. I refer to the talented Col. Kerr. I was close by his side and remember well, when the word came that Col. Childs had fallen, the remark he made, I think to the bearer of the message. Col. Childs sent a request, I believe, that he wished to see Col. Kerr. The Colonel studied a moment and said "No, sir; my place is now with the regiment." From that moment on Col. Kerr rose highly in my estimation as an officer, and I believe did good service thereafter.

It was only this morning that the Major asked me to make some remarks upon Antietam, and asked me to think up something during the day. I will just ask the rest of my comrades whether you have thought of much to-day? That is, whether you had an opportunity to think of much. There was a great deal done; we have all been busy. As the boys say, "I have a big head on me" to-night; I can't account for it. I leave it to Dr. Seip, whom I believe you all know to be a good physician, and understands his business, to judge as to whether it was caused by what I have taken here to-night. (Dr. Seip—The supper ought not to cause it.) Therefore, comrades, thanking you for the kind attention you have given

me, and with the wish that you may enjoy many more such reunions, I bid you good night.

COMRADE JOHN HUSTON:—I rise for a personal explanation, if I am in order. (Major Maitland:—Certainly.)

I would like to say that when I was a small boy I was born of Scotch-Irish, Presbyterian parents. We traced our ancestry back on my father's side to the Bruce family; and I must say that I was taught in my youth to be truthful in all things; but in an evil hour, when I was a small boy, I was apprenticed to the printers' trade, and, like all printers, developed into a most excellent liar. [Laughter.] Why, my dear Major, I was responsible for quite a number of those lies in the *Forest Press*, as I was for some lies in the *Oil City Derrick*. I was a good liar; but, thank God, I never assailed any man's private character in all the lies that ever I was guilty of expressing, nor did I ever assail any community. But here I hold in my hand a copy of a mugwumpian paper published in this city, the *Pittsburgh Dispatch*, wherein I find one of the most amazing lies that I ever saw in my life. They have the audacity to publish, under the title of "Short Stories," a scurrilous account of the Major's life and character during the war. I would like to read it to you, if I can see. When the press stoops to insult an entire brigade, and to villify a good soldier, it is time to call a halt. Now I will read for your edification:

"Major Maitland, of the Fourth, was in the habit of entertaining quite a number of infantry officers—" Now, the idea of it! Entertaining infantry officers at dinner! A lie at the start. It's preposterous! "And the Major had a cook by the name of Hannah—" Did ever any of you gentlemen hear of that Hannah? (Laughter, and cries of "What's the matter with Hannah?") The piece goes on to state that the Major had quite a number of infantry officers around the table, and the spoons fell short—

When he arrived at this point in his speech, the audience was convulsed with laughter and applause, and then

MAJOR MAITLAND arose and responded as follows:

It was an infantry soldier, I believe, whom I heard relate, that, when he first went into the war, he studied and practiced

strategy. Very often when he might have attacked the enemy directly, he made a detour. He had been taught in that
way, and said he, the first time I ever saw an army I was
behind a tree. Well, the enemy was coming directly for that
tree, and I got to one side and to the other side, but the bullets came pecking in, and pecking in, and finally I had to
leave the position. There was a cavalry—(no, I beg pardon,
not a cavalry Chaplain,) but there was a Chaplain there who
also believed in strategy. He wasn't willing to make an open,
direct, straightforward attack. So the Chaplain made a detour,
and this infantry soldier (of course, cavalry wouldn't do that)
made a detour also. But the enemy pressed forward, and
finally one of the Chaplain's limbs was taken off, and one of
the infantry soldier's limbs was taken off also; both lying
there indiscriminately in the road. There was a new surgeon
there, and he, not knowing which belonged to the infantry
soldier and which to the Chaplain, took up the Chaplain's leg
and put it on the infantry soldier, and vice versa. After a
time they came together to celebrate this victory. They were
having a jolly time. The infantry soldier was a man of not
very correct habits; he was like our friend Seip—always sigh-
ing for the canteen or appollinaris, or something of that kind.
He went into one of those little places of business where the
canteen was freely used—(A voice: Speak-easy.) No, sir;
we didn't know anything of that kind; there were no speak-
easies until Pittsburgh introduced them. Well, this infantry
soldier was standing holding a glass in his hand, and was
about to drink to that great victory, when, what should come
up but that foot. The Chaplain's leg protested against that,
and the glass was immediately shaken out of his hand.
[Laughter.] He looked out, and he saw the poor Chaplain
being dragged into that place by the infantry soldier's limb.
[Laughter.] So you will see, both these men were unfortun-
ate, and I have it, upon the best information, that a short time
ago this infantry soldier (who is now a reformed man, and gets
along comfortably well with this limb which is not his own,
but belongs to the Chaplain), went to a prison to talk to the
convicts, and there came out one dressed in prison garb. He
thought he saw something familiar in his face. It was the

former Chaplain. That leg had taken him to State's prison! [Laughter.] Now, I do not vouch for the truth of this story, it was told by an infantry soldier.

I will not answer this newspaper story you have just heard. You know me too well. I know of no Hannah. [Laughter, and a voice: "No, it's a newspaper lie, of course it is!"] The name of the only lady I know is Etta. Now, this matter has been suppressed again and again. In my county I am know as a Prohibitionist, and this story has done me immense injury. I fact, I think it is largely due to this story that I was defeated for the Mayorality on the Prohibition ticket last Spring at Oil City, and I am surprised that a comrade should bring it into this audience as he has to-night and give it further publicity. I want the newspapers to retract it; take it back.

Major Phipps being called upon spoke as follows:

I discover that the Fourth Pennsylvania Cavalry still retains one of its chief characteristics, and that is of pitching into anything it finds. The way you did business the first half hour or so after you came into this room put me a little in mind of Captain Grant. I believe it was on the Kilpatrick, or the Richmond raid, as it was called; we were gone some sixteen days without anything to eat. The Captain captured or had given to him about three gallons of cabbage. He ate it all for dinner and got sick. [Laughter—Voice, " Pickled cabbage!"]

Major Phipps:—Yes, Pickled cabbage.

Comrades, we meet to-night under much different circumstances from that of twenty-six or twenty-seven years ago. Then we were called together by the sound of the bugle. To-night we were called together by the bugle-blast of a "calling-wood" (Collingwood). Always obey that blast when it calls on you and you will have a good time. Comrades, we meet again to-night to reburnish the golden links that bind us together as comrades. I am no speech maker, and I feel very different in the presence of these distinguished guests, and my wife is here. I feel a little to-night in the condition of a comrade of my old command the first fight that we were engaged

in. By-the-way, I presume the comrades remember the screech or sound of the first shell. I do! It was during this engagement, the first shell, or screech of shell that I heard, I made up my mind that it was coming straight for my head. I had charge of the skirmish line; and I wanted to be as brave as possible. I rolled off my horse flat on the ground until I heard the shell explode about a half mile beyond me; when I got up, got my horse, and made up my mind that I would go back to the skirmish line and do my duty. We had one comrade that I could not keep in line; he would be constantly falling back to the rear. About the third time I went to him and said "John, you want to keep up in line, the boys will all begin to call you a coward." He said, " I don't give a d——, my horse is too white to stand up there." That is a little the way with me to-night; my horse is a little too white to make a speech in the presence of these distinguished guests.

As I look into the faces of my old comrades to-night, I can only think of them as the brave, noble boys of one of the grandest regiments that ever marched to the defense of a nation's honor; a regiment composed of men who were always characterized by their undaunted bravery, unflinching courage, and unwavering adherence to the right; possessed with a record resplendent with the noblest achievements of modern warfare; always prepared to do and to die for the eternal right. The history and glorious achivements of the Fourth Pennsylvania Cavalry have been written in letters of light on the pathway of our national history. Its name stands out second to none, tested and tried by the heat and fire of over seventy engagements by the precious blood of its members (our comrades) shed on freedom's altar for liberty and union. By your bravery, courage and noble deeds when your country was in peril, you have erected for yourselves monuments more lasting than brass, and higher than the royal structure of the pyramids. Union now, and forever, one and inseparable was your motto; infallible patriotism was your strength; immutable fortitude your support; your lofty watch-words, Philanthrophy, Fraternity and Equality; your inspiration the grand old stars and stripes that you followed from Drainesville to Appomattox, from victory to victory, until you at last saw it

purified, redeemed and saved, so that to-night it floats out to the breeze majestic and grand, honored and respected by every nation, and in every clime beneath the sun. My comrades, the proudest moments of our lives was when after the din and smoke of the battle had rolled away at Appomattox, our exultant voices joined in the grand old anthem: "The Star Spangled Banner"; stainless and sacred as it ever shall be, we brought it back without the loss of a single star. We meet to-night as comrades proud of our old regiment, proud of our record, proud of each other, and of the part we took in one of the greatest struggles for human liberty recorded in the pages of history, either ancient or modern. The world may call us heroes; historians may perpetuate our deeds, but my comrades, let us remember that the acoutrements of war have long since been laid aside, peace has married progress. We have lived to see the golden band of prosperity encircle 43 states in this glorious Union, peace and prosperity crown the nation unparalled in the annals of time. What the world needs to-day is a progressive philanthropic people. We have been soldiers and patriots, but above all let us be magnanamous American citizens and may it be our inspiration to place one more impregnable rock upon our national structure, and as it rests there throughout the ages, what shall we have it represent, Liberty? No! for that was built into its very foundations by the patriots of the revolution. Patriotism? No! for that has been rolled there by the immortal heroes of Yorktown and Appomattox. Mutual beneficense? Yes! there is the place for that mighty rock, it will crown the summit of our mighty structure and cast a halo of glory and peace over all people. Do this, and we will leave behind us footprints on the sands of time that can never be washed away by the storms of the ages to come; an irreproachable reputation and a character that the world will cherish and admire forever. My comrades what can I say of the immortal heroes, our noble comrades, once with us but now are no more; It seems to me my poor speech would be inadequate for the task of expressing our feelings in regard to them, our noble dead; we remember them as comrades, we remember them in the camp, on the long and dusty marches, in the desperate

battle and deadly strife, in storms of shot and shell, and in the terrible charge, their sabers gleaming in the sun; we remember their last parting words to loved ones as their noble young lives went out on the field of carnage, their heroic blood making rich the land we love, and brighter the red stripes of that old flag they followed to the death; their names would make a long list of heroes to be added to those that are silently sleeping on fame's eternal camping ground. Could we call the roll of our comrade heroes, we would find the names of the gallant Childs—revered by all; the brave, noble Covode; a Duncan, a Mays, a Welton, a Harper, a Phipps; and a host of others whose names have been written in azure with letters of diamonds on the pages of our country's history. They have long since passed into the realms of peaceful slumber, immortalized by the splendor of their matchless conduct and bravery on every battlefield in which they were engaged. They have long since passed within the veil, but we still remember their comradeship and their matchless bravery; let us cherish their memories and emulate their virtues, with the unfailing hope that after life's work is over, crowned with the imperishable chaplet of duty and labor well done, we shall meet them on celestial shores of eternal rest, amid brighter scenes, in happier realms of eternal joy.

After tendering our genial host, Mr. B. C. Willson, a vote of thanks for his liberality and special efforts in making this one of the most enjoyable reunions held in this city, the comrades, after a general hand-shaking, adjourned to meet in Butler at our next reunion.

90

REMINISCENCES.

October 11th we encamped for the night on our old grounds at Sulphur Springs, where on the eventful morning of October 12th, 1863, we crossed over on the north side of · the Rappahannock, halting between Warrenton and Sulphur Springs. We were preparing to go into camp when "Boots and Saddles" was sounded, and we were soon on the march back to Sulphur Springs. Crossing the river, we proceeded to Jefferson, where we found the Thirteenth Penn'a. engaged with Stuart's Cavalry. Our regiment was soon deployed and engaged with the enemy. Towards evening the Rebs closed in on us from all points— infantry and cavalry—the whole of Ewell's Corps being present. They came charging upon us in front and on both flanks, we were driven back and almost surrounded; but I am proud to record the fact, that our small force fought with desperate resistance against such tremendous odds. Several daring charges were made by portions of our regiment. A number of both regiments succeeded in reaching the river at different points, and dashing into the water, made their escape. Many of us however were not so fortunate. In order to keep the road open to the river, those who were mounted made repeated charges along its banks.

While in the act of making the last of these, I was severely wounded. The ball entered my right ear, and, as I afterward learned, came out at the back of my head. I dropped insensible from my horse, and did not become conscious until the enemy, some time after, began to rifle my person, they took my boots, hat and all that was in my pockets. After being taken back a short distance, I found nearly three hundred of our men whom the enemy had captured. Thirteen of these were comrades of my own company and out of this number but few are alive to-day; the rest having died at Libby or Andersonville. The members of our company (A) who were

captured were as follows: Orderly Sergt. Welton; Commissary Sergt. McLaughlin; Privates Boyd, Fritz, Schultz, Moyer, Stahler, Ward, Smith and myself. We arrived in Richmond on the 15th, and were confined in a large tobacco warehouse, denominated "Libby Prison, No. 4." Here we first experienced prison life. The bill of fare consisted of half a pound of corn bread a day to each man, and very seldom any meat.

Obliged to carry our own rations, (such as we received,) every day to the prison, we got a breath of fresh air. A detail of 40 or 50 was made from among the prisoners each day, who, with pieces of old blankets, proceeded under a rebel escort to the bake house, the rations were thrown into these old blankets and carried to the prison. The dead house was adjacent to the commissary department, thus we passed the ghastly charnel of our dead comrades daily, and glanced at it with heavy hearts, we felt that our own emaciated bodies would soon be numbered among its corpses. Having decided to make my escape, and not caring to have more than one companion in the perilous undertaking, I proposed my plan to all the members of my own company separately, but none of them thought it feasible. I at last found my man in Corporal Alex. Welton, "Co. K," he was eager to make the attempt with me, and knowing him to be brave and prudent, I at once took him into my confidence, and we matured the plan by which we made our escape.

We each succeeded in securing a rebel cap and we already had old, tattered grey jackets, and now felt ready to make the attempt, we got detailed together to assist in carrying rations. Taking our positions about the centre of the column as it moved out of prison in files of two, we each had a piece of blanket around our shoulders, and our rebel caps under our arms; the column was protected by one rebel guard in advance, one in the rear and one Corporal a little forward of the centre. We requested the comrades in our rear to promptly fill the gap in case we stepped out at any point, and also take our blankets. Just as the centre turned the corner of 19th street, so that the rear guard could not see us, leaving the ranks quickly, we donned our rebel caps, started

down Main street again, and passed the rebel guard in the rear very nervously, whistling the "Bonnie Blue Flag," and trying to assume rebel airs. We quickened our pace in order to turn the next corner soon as possible, and in a short time were at the river, in the vicinity of the Navy-yard. Remaining in this partially secure place for a short time, our nerves became more steady, which gave us renewed courage. Again we started for the suburbs of the city. We walked boldly on until we found ourselves in a small ravine about five miles from the city limits; here we seated ourselves behind a pile of cord-wood, and then for the first time, ventured to open our hearts to each other, and to congratulate ourselves on the success, (thus far) of the undertaking.

After a short rest we proceeded—not knowing whither we were going—and soon met an old negro with an old horse and cart-load of wood. After some hesitation we decided to question him about the roads, and found we were on the direct route to Harrison's Landing, where the enemy's out-posts were located. We told him we were escaping prisoners, when he at once took an interest in our behalf, and gave all the information he could. He advised us to secrete ourselves until night-fall, and to keep clear of all white men, as the whole neighborhood were in league in order to re-capture escaping prisoners—but, said he, "you need not fear the colored people, they are your friends," and such they proved to be. After parting with our colored friend, we concealed ourselves in underbrush near the road-side until it became quite dark. A short time after a very heavy rain and wind storm set in, the rain coming down in torrents. Onward we sped, Welton grasping my wrist, and thus we hurried along with drooping heads, yet with faintly hopeful hearts, our minds intent on thought. Not a word was exchanged during the entire night. With all its terrors, such a storm was our safeguard.

We arrived at Westover Landing shortly after day-light and concealed ourselves in an old deserted house on the river bank. Secreting ourselves among a lot of corn fodder which we found therein, and being very tired, slept soundly until late in the afternoon. While sitting on the river bank we discovered a boat fastened to a pier, we concluded to

make this boat our means of escape down the river. Feeling very hungry we crawled up to one of the plantation buildings and discovered a darkey in the yard, whom I recognized as one I had met during the encampment of our army at Harrison's Landing. He at once took us inside, and after hearing our story, gave us all he had to eat, consisting of a week's rations of corn-meal, which he made into cakes, and a small piece of shoulder, we did not stop until we devoured his entire week's allowance. It was now quite dark, after bidding our colored friend good bye, we at once started for the boat previously referred to.

Soon we were in the middle of the James River, silently pursuing our course. It was a cold November night, we were in a leaky boat, bare footed and very thinly clad, but we were seeking our liberty, and these were but as naught. Becoming quite fatigued toward morning, we approached the shore feeling that we had passed the most of our dangers, we landed near the mouth of the Chickahominy; after a thorough search we failed to find a single habitation, returning, we sat down on the cold, damp shore, and huddling together, shivered as if we had been seized with congestive chills, encircling each other, we lay down in still increasing misery and suffering. Through fatigue, slumber came upon us, we awoke to find the sun shining bright and clear, we found it almost impossible to rise, being so stiffened and benumed; we again entered our boat, and after an eventful ride of several hours we landed, abandoning our boat, and taking a direction, as we thought, toward Williamsburg we soon struck a road, shortly came to where it forked, where we found a mile-post which pointed toward Williamsburg, five miles distant, and, after five long hours of agony, we reached our picket line, and were taken to the provost-marshall's; next day we were conveyed to Fort Mc-Gruder, where we received every attention. After a few days recuperation, we were taken to Fortress Monroe, and at once conveyed to Gen. Meredith's headquarters; he supplied us with everything necessary from the Quartermaster's Department. The following day we were sent to a camp of distribution at Baltimore. I applied for and was granted a furlough; Welton preferred being sent at once to the regiment.

94

RECOLLECTIONS OF COMRADE H. CRAWFORD,
RELATIVE TO THE DEATH OF COL. JAMES H. CHILDS.

Will give you my idea of this occurrence. When we filed to the left of the road after crossing the bridge in support of the battery in front of us, (name of the battery does not occur to me) there was Companies B. and M. commanded by S. B. M. Young, and Companies E. and A. I think, commanded by Capt. Tumbler, (am not positive about Company E.)

Capt. Tumbler was sent with us to place Tidball's battery at the right of the road at the top of the hill. We had the fence partly torn down and two guns up the bank, and I was lifting on a wheel of one of the pieces, when the rebel battery commenced shelling us. The first shot they fired, hit a dead tree just to the left of the road in front of us. The second shot came down among us, did not explode, but wounded John Irvin, of Co. B. The third shot came down to business, passed under my horse, cut both legs off of my brother Geo. W. Crawford's horse, and killed the next man and horse to him. Sergt. Cramer, of Co. M. was the man killed. The same shot also wounded John Boyce, of Co. B., in the foot. This raised a commotion among us. I took Boyce on my back and when about half way down the hill, our Colonel was hit. I did not stop with my man, but crossed the bridge about fifty yards to a house on the right of the road, where a hospital was being established. When I got back to the regiment they told me the Colonel was dead. When we afterwards advanced over the same road, the spot was plain to be seen where our Colonel had lain on the bank of the road, and we all spoke of the occurence. That morning after we advanced almost to the river, we formed in line and Capt. Herron, of Co. E, rode out in front of the regiment, held up his discharge, told what it was, said "good-bye" and left.

I saw a map of this field, and the location where Col. Childs was killed. It was very correct all but the spot, and it was in the rear of the regiment where we formed on the left of the road. Howe Childs had the map and he wanted to locate

the spot where his father was killed. He took two men and went there, the place where they located it, I claim it is not correct. Conversed with several of the comrades and they did not know the exact spot.

Referring to recollections of Comrade Crawford, relative to the death of Col. Childs, I would say that I concur heartily in his statement, and that writers that claim that he was under cover of the hill, pleasantly chatting with companions, are in error. When the fatal missile struck him he was near the crest of the hill, on horseback, returning to the command, after reconnoitering the position in front, and accompanied by a member of his staff, Capt. H. M. Hughes, of Co. K. The Adjutant, who was temporarily in command of Co. G., supporting the battery, saw the Colonel at the moment he was stricken down, and the sad news soon spread, and he remembers with one impulse "G" started to the rescue of their beloved leader, and it was with the utmost difficulty they where restrained from breaking away from their position. The sadness of that hour was only equaled by that, of when the news of the death of Lincoln came to us. Of commanding presence, courteous and affable, he won the hearts of officers and men alike.—*Adjutant.*

L. C. DARTE, OF CO. M., CONTRIBUTES THE FOLLOWING RELATING TO COLONEL COVODE.

WILKES-BARRE, PA., March 10th, 1890.

I have often thought that if Colonel Covode had not been so utterly regardless at all times of his own personal safety, he might have passed through the war. This of course is only one of those suggestive thoughts that will arise in one's mind under circumstances past. I recall in my own memory the regard he had for others by a little incident which I, myself, recollect "awful well" as the little girl would say.

It was sometime in May 1864, I think the very day of the fight at "Yellow Tavern," the day that Gen. Jeb. Stuart was

killed, that I was acting as one of Col. Covode's "orderlies," I rode after him and with him all that day. Our brigade was confronted, I think, by the rebel Gen. Gordon's cavalry.

Col. Covode rode away from where our regiment was drawn up in line, out to the edge of the proverbial "clump of trees" which skirted an open field, and I, as "orderly," of course followed. It was some distance from the regiment, right before us, and within three or four hundred feet—possibly it was some distance more than three or four hundred feet— one or Gordons' regiments was just forming into line of regimental front. We looked at them as they posted their guidons and galloped into line. Of course Col. Covode had halted as soon as he discovered them and there he sat on his horse and I on mine, a little to his rear and side. It did not appear to be but a minute or two since we had halted our horses, when zip, zip, zip, sung the bullets as they whizzed passed us.

The zip, zip, of the little missiles came in quick and continuous succession. The firing was from another quarter and not from the men of the regiment fronting us. Col. Covode never moved. It suggested to my mind at the time that the rebel regiment opposite us were on dress-parade and Col. Covode as its commanding officer was reviewing them. The firing became so hot that the horses themselves grew restless under it, especially mine. Possibly its rider was just a little restless too; but the Col. showed not the slighest inclination to get away from the position. I looked at him very earnestly and very intently. He had on his face htat peculiar but pleasant looking smile, which to this day is as vividly fixed in my memory as if it was but yesterday I had seen it. The zipping sounds of the little leaden messengers seemed to increase every moment, yet Col. Covode remained in the exposed position watching carefully every movement of the rebel regiment in our front.

As the firing directed to us seemed to increase he turned his smiling face to me, and never thinking of himself, said "Darte, it's a hot place here for you, you can fall back if you choose." Darte didn't fall back, for the order was somewhat qualified, but was awfully willing to "get out of that" soon as possible all the same.

97

Just about this time, however, one of our light battery guns—I think Capt. Robinson's battery—opened up from a point on our left on that little rebel regiment in front of us and the rapidity with which they "got out of that" was both gratifying and amusing. Col. Covode smiled, for he had reviewed a rebel regiment apparently on dress-parade, and apparently dismissed them. Of course all this is only a little incident, and possibly uninteresting in detail, but together with other like matters connected with the character of Col. Covode, gave to me an insight into his character which will always remain with me.

I have the highest regard for his memory, in his every way of doing things, as I recollect them, in the years gone by.

COPY OF LETTER FROM GENERAL D. McM. GREGG,.
DECEMBER, 1889.

How well I remember the gallant Colonel Covode. At the moment we were compelled to abandon him, I was with the rear guard, and in falling back came upon the party bearing their Colonel on a stretcher. His great weight and the intense heat made it impossible for the men to carry him farther. I dismounted, and from a small flask gave him some brandy, but the rebels were close upon us, and the Colonel, careful of the safety of others, had bade me leave him else I would be captured. At the last moment I quit him most sorrowfully. He was a grand soldier.

"DEEP BOTTOM, AUGUST 16, 1864."
LEAVES FROM THE DIARY OF MAJ. J. B. MAITLAND, A. A. G.

Orders at a few minutes after midnight to march at 4 A. M. In accordance with the same, the regiments and section of battery were notified, and at 5 A. M. moved in the following order: 16th Penn'a; 1st Maine; Section 8th Penn'a; 13th Penn'a; the 4th and 2nd Penn'a on picket duty.

We struck the Charles City road at an early hour, withdrew 4th and 2nd Penn'a from picket line, and the 4th Penn'a

previously ordered on Central Road, was halted and awaited the coming of the brigade. Arriving within gun-shot of the enemy's rifle-pits at Deep Run. The 2nd and 4th were thrown across the stream and dismounted, completely routing the enemy. The 16th Penn'a. then charged, and the A. A. G. was directed to bring rapidly forward, one gun; which did not arrive in time to open on the retreating foe. The entire command was moved forward and the advance led in person by Col. Gregg, became warmly engaged. The Colonel was wounded in the wrist while in the extreme advance. His loss at that time was keenly felt; not only by the members of the staff, but by the entire brigade, as his place could not be well filled, he having the whole plan of battle well matured.

The command devolved on Col. Kerwin, of the 13th, being the senior officer present. As the head of the column moved on to the attack, Col. Gregg said, (pointing to the wounded arm) "tell the boys to avenge this."

Soon after, the body of Gen. Chambliss was brought back. Truly, we thought, is our brave leader avenged. Afterwards the body of the Rebel General was sent under flag of truce, within the rebel lines.

The enemy were driven, with but slight resistance, to a point on the road about one and one-half miles from White's where they were found strongly entrenched and in some force. Soon they opened a brisk fire, principally on the road, to prevent our further advance. Only two shots from their battery. We soon found they were outflanking us in a movement to our left, which caused our line to fall back.

Although closely pressed and under a severe fire, we formed in an open space and held the enemy in check. Here was wounded the gallant Lieut. Mattson, seriously; also Lieut. Cutler, slightly; and Col. Kerwin's life saved by a diary; the ball intended for his heart, penetrating the diary which he had in a side pocket. The shock, however, was sufficiently severe to disable him from further service, and for the second time on that eventful day, we were without a leader.

Forming a second line, we gradually withdrew from the first. The second line we were directed to maintain at all hazards, and nobly the Cavalry did it.

99

Although mounted and formed on the crest of a hill, receiving volley after volley of musketry, still they stood until the welcome orders came to fall back to yet another line, which was accomplished in good order under an artillery as well as musketry fire. The 2nd Penn'a. had formed a line in the edge of the woods fronting the plain on the banks of Deep Run, behind which we formed. Soon our skirmishers were driven in upon the main body and finding our position untenable—the enemy having gained posession of the woods—we again fell back, crossing the swamp, and taking posession there we held it during the remainder of the day. We lost heavily in this action. Among the fallen brave, none were more deeply lamented than Geo. McCoy, Co. L., 4th Penn'a. His comrades brought off the body, exposing themselves to a severe fire while doing so; and burried it on Charles City road in the presence of many who dearly loved him for his many soldierly qualifications and manly virtues. Lieut. Geo. L. Bragg, fell by a stray bullet, a noble, brave officer, ever at his post, and unlike some others, filling a like position, usually accompanied his command to the front. Among the wounded were Lieut. Col. Wilson, Maj. W. A. Corrie, Lieut. Orton Reed, Lieut. Nellis, Lieut. Robeson and Capt. Hall.

A number of narrow escapes, a number of officers having their clothing riddled with bullets, yet receiving no serious harm; no special mention can be made where all behaved with the most praiseworthy coolness and gallantry. At a late hour we were relieved by the first brigade, when we returned to camp, drew three days rations and a supply of amunition.

August 17th, in camp, except a detachment sent on scout to Turkey Bridge and Malvern Hill. August 18th, heavy skirmishing along Steadman's line. 4th Penn'a dismounted and marched to the breastworks. Two men killed by a shell which passed through the column. Loss heavy in men and horses since crossing the James River, August 14th. August 19th, in camp. August 20th, withdrew pickets at dark and re-crossed the James and Appomattox Rivers.

August 21st, breakfasted near Prince George, C. H., then moved to left of army on Jerusalem plank road. After a few

hours rest, at early moonlight moved to Gurley House and bivouacked, 4th Penn'a on picket, relieved afternoon of 22nd by 13th Penn'a. August 23rd, marched at 8 A. M. in direction of Ream's Station, on Weldon R. R. and found infantry busily engaged destroying rails and ties.

A high compliment, and appreciated accordingly :

HEADQUARTERS 2D BRIGADE, 2D CAVALRY DIV.,
CAVALRY CORPS, ARMY OF THE POTOMAC,
NOVEMBER 20TH, 1864.

GENERAL ORDER,
No. 109.

At the Sunday inspection of Quarters, the camp of the Fourth Pennsylvania Cavalry exhibited so marked a superiority in the arrangement of company quarters, general police of camp, neatness and cleanliness of the men, as to indicate a commendable attention to the details of the service on the part of the officers.

(Signed)   J. IRVIN GREGG,

JOHN B. MAITLAND,   B't. Brig. Gen. Com. Brigade.

Capt. and A. A. G.

HEADQUARTERS 2ND BRIGADE, 2ND DIV., C. C.,
ARMY OF THE POTOMAC,
BEFORE PETERSBURG, VA., NOV. 23RD, 1864.

GENERAL ORDER,
No. 14.

SOLDIERS OF THE 2ND BRIGADE, 2ND DIVISION CAVALRY CORPS:—

Your fellow citizens of Pennsylvania have presented to you through me, as a testimonial of their appreciation of your services to your country, a battle flag.

It was my desire that the flag should have been presented direct to you, but the exigencies of the service required your services, and you could not be assembled as a brigade. The flag has been presented to your officers for you, and I feel confident that you will recognize the necessity which forbade its presentation to you direct.

101

The history written upon its standard, is your history. All the honor or glory that may attach to the names inscribed upon the standard is your glory, for you have made these names memorable by your endurance and your chivalric courage.

Confidently, then, it is committed to your care, with the proud assurance, that whilst your strong arms can strike, it will be carried from victory to victory until the hideous monster of rebellion is annihilated, and peace again reigns supreme over our once happy land.

(Signed)   J. IRVIN GREGG,

(Official.)   Col. Com. Brigade and B't. Brig Gen.

JOHN B. MAITLAND,
     Capt. and A. A. G.

HEADQUARTERS 4TH PENN'A CAVALRY, }
PITTSBURGH, PA., JULY 8TH, 1865. }

OFFICERS AND MEMBERS OF THE FOURTH PENN'A. CAVALRY:—

In parting with you, who have gallantly performed your duties in defence of the Union, your commanding officer deems it necessary to say it is with reluctance. From the organization of the regiment he has officiated with you in various capacities. His positions have been such, that his acquaintance with each one as a soldier in camp as also in the field, has been personal, creating an attachment, that is now about to be severed, but never forgotten. For four years your life has been his, the privations and hardships which you have suffered, he has also endured, but the recompense has been a full compensation. By your gallantry and daring, on every battle field, you have won the admiration of the whole country. You have wrested from the hands of arch traitors, the proud emblem of liberty.

You have once more opened the doors of the free institutions of a powerful people, and firmly established the great fundamental principle that there is no such thing as secession, but by hydra-headed treason, and punishable to the full extent

by millitary law; and not only that, but you have also established the supremacy of "The Star Spangled Banner" above all nations of the world.

Among the officers of this command, your commander sees none in the same capacity in which they entered the service. You have been promoted to your present respective grades for gallant and meritorious services rendered on many fields of "gore." You have by your deportment won the full confidence and esteem of your commander. And for your assistance and obedience to all orders, he thanks you.

And now that your country no longer requires your services, beat your swords into plow shares and your spears into pruning hooks, that the clanking of arms may no longer salute the ear, but be superseded by the busy hum of industry. Let your deportment hereafter be in accordance with your military life, and prove to the world that a soldier can be a good citizen; that he who raises the arm to establish law, also raises it for its maintenance.

You will soon gather around your hearth-stones, and recount your perils, privations, hardships and sufferings, to the loved ones at home, but your bosoms will always heave with emotions of pride in the exclamation, I was a soldier of the Union. Your name will be revered by the loyal, the great and the good.

For our comrades who have fallen, we shed a tear ; our sympathies go forth to the house of mourning, and would condole with the afflicted.

Their loss has been in a glorious cause, the propitiation of freedom to you and to all posterity.

We shall soon separate, perhaps never to meet again, but your memories will be the proudest of my recollections, to be erased only by the soul's exit.

S. B. M. YOUNG,
B't. Brig. Gen. Vols. and Col. 4th Penn'a. Cavalry.

A complimentary letter to the Fourth Penn'a Cavalry:

103

LYNCHBURG, VA., JULY 1ST, 1865.

OFFICERS AND SOLDIERS OF THE FOURTH PENN'A CAVALRY:

After four years of war, the most terrible the world ever saw, you are about to return to your homes, your friends and your families, with the object for which you left your fields and your workshops, your pleasant homes, your wives and your little ones, accomplished. Peace again spreads her wings over our entire country, and let us hope it will be over a united and a happy people. Soldiers, soon to become citizens, carry with you to your homes, and into your various occupations and pursuits, the lessons you have learned, of courage, of endurance, of fortitude, of generoisity, of magnanimity. Let no unworthy views contract or occupy your minds. Show to your recent enemies that the contest for the past four years has not embittered your hearts.

Bear in mind that your comrades sleep, side by side in a common grave, with a gallant but mistaken foe; that what we have done was from a sense of duty and justice, and not in a spirit of wanton aggression or of unbridled passion. Go, soldiers of the Fourth Pennsylvania Cavalry, to be happy with, and to render happy, those whom you love and cherish. We may never meet again, but the rememberance of your gallant deeds and heroic endurance will never fade from the memory of him who has had the honor to lead you through the trials and dangers of the past, and he trusts that you will carry with you kind memories of one, who, whatever may have been his faults or his failures, has striven to do his duty, and gloried in the leadership of a command whose achievements are second to none. May God bless you, and keep you as pure citizens as you have been faithful soldiers.   J. IRVIN GREGG,

Brev. Brig. Gen. Vols.

Extract from letter of General J. IRVIN GREGG in response to invitation to Gettysburg Reunion :—

It will afford me pleasure to meet again on the memorable battle-field of 1863, the officers and men of the Fourth Penn'a. after so many years. Doubtless we will all see changes that time has brought to each of us in personal appearance, but the

affections will always remain green, for who can forget the friendships formed amid the stirring scenes through which we have passed, on the march, in the bivouac, and in the deadly strife of many a hotly contested field. Yes, my heart goes out toward the men of the Fourth Cavalry, and I wish for them the fullest measure of prosperity in this life and happiness of the future.

NOTE.—Truly time had wrought changes in personal appearance, for the General failed to recognize his old A. A. G., and when made known to him, said: "Well old man, how are you?" It is tough, boys, to be designated an "old man;" but we, or many of us, must recognize its appropriateness.

The deeds of the regiment recited in verse by J. A. Morrison, (120 verses) is unfortunately too lengthy to be given in full, but we append a sample:—

> "Come all surviving comrades, and listen while I tell
> About the many battles in which we fought so well,
> From eighteen hundred and sixty-one to eighteen sixty-five,
> With many who are "missing" and some who are alive.
>
> Commencing May the seventeeth, in eighteen sixty-two,
> When we were "recent" volunteers and everything was new,
> We were ordered out of camp to guard the Crowning Ridge,
> And our glory thus began at the battle of Bottom's Bridge.
> * * * * * * * *
> The ninth of April, sixty-five, heard shouts of freemen rise
> Far above Lee's veterans in the Appomattox skies,
> For, at last the end had come, and long to be remembered,
> When Robert E. Lee to U. S. Grant had surrendered."

COMRADE H. D. HACKNEY, (Co. D,) Walton Post, 243, Department Kansas, G. A. R., April 10, 1891, writes as follows:

I am an outcast, as it were, from members of my regiment, having come West in 1868, and have seen but two or three since. I am one of Uncle Sam's pensioners from injuries received at Hawes' Shop and Warwick Swamp. I had the honor to capture and disarm the officer, (a Major, I think,) who commanded the Fort at Stony Creek Station, December 1st, 1864, where our regiment did a good breakfast job!

I often wish I was where I could mingle with my old comrades, and recount the scenes of those days,—for while we have, no doubt, as brave and genial "boys" here—still, "as Si says of Shorty,—he was my pard.

105

A PITTSBURGHER'S DIARY.

Senator Hill, of Georgia, Confronted by a Diary Record of Life in Libby Prison.

Very few men, says the New York *Press*, came out of Libby prison with a diary in which were recorded the daily events of prison life from the day of their incarceration until the period of confinement closed. The *Press* happened to come upon one of the few exceptions last week in the person of John Fulton, Jr., of the drug importing firm of Stallman & Fulton on Gold street, this city. He started a diary after his capture and faithfully recorded every-day experiences during an imprisonment of seven months in Richmond.

Mr. Fulton is a native of Pittsburgh, and was for many years engaged in the wholesale drug house of B. L. Fahnestock & Co., on Wood street. He left the employ of the firm when the war broke out, and enlisted in Company G, Fourth Pennsylvania Cavalry, first commanded by Col. Campbell, and afterward by Col. Childs, both of Pittsburgh, the latter was killed at Antietam. The regiment was subsequently commanded by Col. George H. Covode, who was killed at St. Mary's Church.

The small memorandum book kept by Mr. Fulton is highly prized by the owner, as it not only refreshes his memory concerning the eventful past, but it has played an important part in a heated discussion between James G. Blaine and the late Senator Hill on the floor of the United States Senate, as will be seen by the following account given by the New York *Press*.

General Morgan, the celebrated confederate raider, while a prisoner in Columbus, O., had heard considerable complaint about the treatment of Union prisoners at Richmond, and he resolved to see justice done at the first opportunity. After his escape from the penitentiary, in the latter part of 1863, he commenced an investigation, and would not be satisfied until the leading representatives of the Confederate government

accompanied him on a tour of the southern prisons. The commission of investigation was composed of himself, Jefferson Davis, General Ben Hill, John Mitchell, the famous Irishman and then editor of a Richmond daily paper, and several other prominent persons.

Mr. Fulton was acting as ward master of the prison hospital, on Cary and Twenty-second streets, which was in charge of Dr. Hopkins, who had the title of major. When the distinguished visitors called on their tour of investigation January 9, 1864, it devolved upon Mr. Fulton to escort them through the hospital. Gen. Morgan made earnest inquiries about the treatment of patients, and the latter invariably asked for more food, which provoked Jeff Davis to remark: "Did you ever know a Yankee to be satisfied?" It was found that the hospital had been without fire or fuel during the entire season and that the inmates had been living on one-third of the required rations. At that time the James river was nearly frozen over, and the weather was said to have been the coldest for 20 years.

Gen. Morgan preferred charges against the commissary department as a result of the tour, and the subsequent official inquiry disclosed the fact that the quarter master had appropriated to his own use the money paid by the confederate government for the care of Union prisoners. He was relieved from duty, and when a senate committee visited the Richmond prisons the improvement was very noticeable.

At the time that Senator Hill had a wordy tussle with James G. Blaine, and the latter found it necessary to make his famous speech in the senate, the circumstances, as related above, proved to be good ammunition in the hands of Mr. Blaine. The little bit of history was transcribed from Mr. Fulton's diary, sworn to before a notary, and given in charge of Hon. Amos Clark, Jr., who was then serving his second term as congressman from the Third New Jersey district. He carried the affidavit to Washington and tendered it to Mr. Blaine, who was profuse in his thanks for such valuable material, as it answered his opponent better than any other argument.

107

Senator Hill did not expect to see an eye witness to come forward to testify to the result of the tour made by the investigating committee through the Richmond prisons, and having been a member of that commission his fiery speech failed to have the desired effect when Mr. Blaine secured a reading and read a few lines from his tell-tale diary. Hon. Amos Clark, who performed the mission for Mr. Fulton, is a prominent resident of Elizabeth, N. J. He was a great admirer of Gen. Grant, and was itimately associated with him during the latter's adminstration in Washington.

Mr. Fulton was sergeant of Co. G., Fourth Pennsylvania Cavalry, and was captured on October 12, 1863, at Jefferson, near Culpepper, Va. by Maj. Jones, of the Twelfth Virginia Cavalry, during the retreat of Gen. Meade to Manassas for new lines of defence. His first recollection of Libby prison was, when in a line of unfortunates waiting for a description to be taken, the newcomers where greeted with a cry of "fresh fish" from comrades then in confinement at Mayo's tobacco factory on Main street, where the cavalry were assigned, the infantry going to Belle island. When Gen. Mosby's men were captured and shot for their inhuman depredations it was announced that the confederacy would retaliate by shooting the same number of prisoners.

One day an officer went through the prison calling out the name of John Fulton, and thinking that he had been selected as a victim for revenge, the bearer of the name, then under 21 years of age, remained silent until assured of better treatment. When making known his presence he was asked to serve as ward master of the hospital, as he had a thorough knowledge of drugs. He remained in that position until Feb. 21, 1864, when Maj. Hopkins in charge transferred him to the dispensary, where he compounded from 200 to 300 prescriptions daily from 7 A. M. to 11 P. M. Having given strict attention to his duties in helping others to prolong life, he was promised transportation north with the first exchange of prisoners, but his services were so valuable that Maj. Hopkins positively refused to release him, stating that he could accomplish more good there among his fellowmen than at the north.

108

He saw a crowd of 600 infirm prisoners leave for home without him, and that made him concoct a scheme for escape, as he did not intend to remain there as a "Yankee nest egg," as Dr. Hopkins was pleased to term him. Mr. Fulton had been reduced in weight from 145 to 98 pounds, and was gradually wasting away from lack of proper food, hard work and anxiety. His successor in the hospital, James Furlong by name, and hailing from Michigan, assisted in the escape by having the name of his comrade entered on the list of those eligible for dismissal. As only those incapacitated for duty were released, Mr. Fulton had to assume a disguise and be examined for chronic spine disease, which he passed satisfactorily, and was assisted into an ambulance by the same Dr. Hopkins who refused to let him go, and who supposed that he was then in the hospital attending to his duties.

Comrade Fulton has promised the Publishing Committee some very interesting items from his diary, for publication in our next volume of Regimental History.

ONE OF THE BOYS IN CIVIL LIFE.

A meeting of Encampment No. 45, Union Veteran Legion. Butler, Pa., was held at the hall of the order, in the Reiber building, on Thursday evening of last week, to which the public were invited. Besides members of the Encampment and many citizens, a large detachment from St. Paul's Orphan Home was present.

The evening passed pleasantly, enlivened by patrotic songs, in which the well-tuned voices of the orphans heartily joined, and short speeches by members and guests.

Interest culminated however, in the announcement and execution of a sentence pronounced upon Major R. J. Phipps, late Commander of the Encampment. The Major was called to the front, and stood with bared head before Post Commander F. M. Eastman, who addressed him as follows:

"This is a serious matter. You have been tried and found guilty by a court martial of your comrades. The trial was a star chamber proceeding. You were not notified, neither were

you served with a copy of the charges and specifications. But your presence would not have changed the result. You were ably defended by the Judge Advocate. The indictment contains but a single charge—a single specification. Charge: False pretense. Specification: On or about the 27th day of June, 1889, and at divers times since, continuing down to January 13, 1891, the date of trial, you did represent that you were nothing but a plain, ordinary, common cavalryman, which is not correct.

"Your record before the war we have heard from your own lips. Your record since the war is well known by almost every citizen of Western Pennsylvania. By your upright honorable course in civil life, you have won the respect and esteem of all who know you. Your record as presiding officer, barring this one instance, has been good. You have been found guilty, and it only remains to pronounce sentence and carry it into execution.

"There was considerable discussion about the kind of punishment. One suggested that you be blown from the muzzle of a cannon; but we do not possess a cannon. Another that you be shot to death with musketry; we don't own a single musket. That you be run through with a calvary sabre; through the generosity of the Army of the Cumberland we have the sword of the famous guerilla chieftain, John Morgan, captured and presented to this encampment by Comrade George Shaffer; but, sir, you are too good a man to be pierced by rebel steel. Like the Mikado of Japan, the Court was determined 'to make the punishment fit the crime.'

"Inasmuch as your extreme modesty was one great cause of your offence, a double punishment has been prescribed. The first part will now be administered, the balance later on. The first part is that your correct military record be read before this assembly :—Robert J. Phipps, enlisted Oct. 14, 1861, as private in Co. H., 4th Penn'a Cavalry. Promoted to First Sergeant. Promoted to Second Lieutenant, March 1, 1863. Promoted to First Lieutenant, March 23, 1863. Promoted to Captain, August 1, 1864. Promoted to Major, March 7, 1865. Brevetted Lieutenant Colonel, March 13, 1865. Discharged,

110

July 1, 1865, by reason of the end of the war. It is but proper
to say that you were brevetted Lieutenant Colonel upon the
personal recommendation of General Philip H. Sheridan. Now
comes the most desperate part of the punishment. Will Misses
Kinter and Geyer, soldier's orphans from St. Paul's Home,
please come forward and assist in this painful duty.

"Now, sir, it becomes my exceedingly great pleasure in
the name and behalf of Encampment No. 45, Union Veteran
Legion, to direct these young ladies to decorate your manly
breast with this beautiful badge. Wear it as a slight token of
the esteem, honor—aye, love of your comrades of Encampment No. 45, Union Veteran Legion."

The badge presented was of beautiful design, and of solid
gold. The gallant Major, who is a fluent and forcible speaker
when not taken at a disadvantage, expressed his thanks in
very few words.

The Brevet Colonelcy which crowned his military rank
was recommended by General Sheridan "for gallantry on the
field of battle."

SURGEON J. S. SKEELS, writes as follows:

MY DEAR COMRADES:—It is with pleasure that I write
you in regard to our past soldier life, you will bear with me
because I am now old and crippled.

It would be impossible for me to relate stories of mirth;
my lot and position in the army was of such a nature as to cast
a cloud over the beautiful sunshine, and make the heart nearly
melt with grief over the misery, pain and anguish of our
beloved soldiers, as they were brought from the battle-field
where they had fallen in defence of their Country. When my
mind reverts back to that time, I can imagine that I see the
soldier, bleeding and dying, his life ebbing and passing away;
others with their limbs broken, others wounded through their
mortal body in all manner of forms, and I myself engaged in
dressing these various wounds and caring for the sick and
afflicted. When I think of the loss of the many brave soldiers
who have fallen in defence of their Country, my mind rests
for a while on that of Major Mays, who lost his life at Farm-

ville; perhaps I might say no braver soldier ever faced the rebel bullets than he, no truer man to his country for which he died, no better man to the soldiers under his command; he died as he lived, kind hearted, and yet brave. There are many others of whom I might write, did space permit.

While sickness, sorrow, death and the cold grave has closed over our loved comrades, obedient sons of loyalty, affectionate husbands, dear fathers, and filial brothers; then you understand as the God-given arch on the cloud is born of sunshine and of storm, so our present and most hallowed joys sometimes span the vale of deepest sorrow.

My comrades, may the day be far distant when our altars shall cease to bear the lights of perpetual brotherhood; far distant when the widow and orphan shall appeal in vain for aid at our hands; far distant when the ties of army life shall have been forgotten. May the memory thereof be perpetuated as is the glorious old Fourth day of July 1776, when our fore-fathers declared this country a free and independent nation, and who so bravely fought for seven long years to obtain this American Independence which we enjoy to-day, and have enjoyed for the last one hundred and fourteen years. And let us not forget this great union of states which, as a nation has grown and prospered for about eighty-four years, unmo-lested, and the rights of American Citizenship not denied any-one. And let us now be willing to forgive our erring brethren who attemped to dissolve this great union of states and tear down that glorious old flag which was an emblem of American Liberty and Freedom,—liberty of speech, liberty of thought, and freedom for all true American Citizens. This glorious old flag, handed down to us by our forefathers, was by us protected, although it has been stained by the blood of brothers and used as a winding sheet for the sons of America and a swad-ling cloth for the dying, yet we done honor to our forefathers and protected that flag until now it floats over these United States, honored and respected by all nations, without a single stripe erased, or a single star obscured. It was for the pro-tection of this glorious old flag, and for the preservation of this Union, that we went forth at the call for men, and faced the

enemy amidst flying bullets, thinking more of our country than our lives. And now my comrades the war is over, right has prevailed, the Union of states restored, and we have so nobly preserved the Constitution of the United States, that justice demands that we should be honored for so doing.

I hope I may live to meet with you at future reunions; but, if my time should come to join the host of soldiers who have passed over the River of Jordan, during and since the war, remember me as one who went forth at my country's call, to preserve this glorious Union, and to render such medical assistance to the sick and wounded as my professional skill afforded.

A SUGGESTIVE RECORD.

SHOWING WHAT CAVALRY REGIMENTS DID THE MOST FIGHTING DURING THE WAR.

The following official record of the number of engagements in which the regiments named below participated, in which losses occured, will be found of interest. In each case the figures given are those of the regiment whose official record among the regiments of the State is the highest, as stated in regimental records:

First Maine, 81; Fourth Pennsylvania, 77; Eighth Illinois, 76; Tenth Missouri, 76; First Massachusetts, 72; Second Ohio, 65; Fourth Iowa, 64; Sixth Michigan, 63; First Vermont, 61; First Arkansas, 57; Second Kansas, 56; First West Virginia, 53; Tenth New York, 50; Third Indiana, 50; First Wisconsin, 45; First Maryland, 44; Sixth Kentucky, 35; First New Jersey, 34; First Rhode Island, 27; First Connecticut, 27; Fourth Tennessee, 20.—*National Tribune.*

Seven Company Corresponding Secretaries report a list of 83 additional killed and wounded together with 88 names of comrades not recorded in Bates' History of Pennsylvania Volunteers.

Our next volume will contain Revised Rolls of each Company, including a complete list of the killed, wounded and captured and those who died in prison.

113

COMPANY CORRESPONDING SECRETARIES.

Co. A.—W. J. Boyd, - - - - Mauch Chunk, Pa.

Co. B.—R. H. McMunn, - - - Allegheny, Pa.

Co. C.—J. H. Leasher, - - - Pleasant Unity, Pa.

Co. D.—James Ogden, - - - Latrobe, Pa.

Co. E.—Henry M. Kerr, - - - Boston P. O., Pa.

Co. F.—H. J. Hambleton, - - Philadelphia, Pa.

Co. G.—John W. Moore, - - - Pittsburgh, Pa.

Co. H.—A. M. Beatty, - - - Dempseytown, Pa.

Co. I.—Alex. Frazier, - - Cooperstown, Pa.

Co. K.—J. R. Grant, - - - Franklin, Pa.

Co. L.—Abner J. Pryor, - - - Rockland P. O., Pa.

Co. M.—L. C. Darte, - - - Wilkes-Barre, Pa.

Copies of this book can be had by addressing Capt. W. K. Gillespie, Nos. 52 and 54 Seventh Avenue, Pittsburgh, Pa. Price 75 cents per copy.

www.ingramcontent.com/pod-product-compliance
Lightning Source LLC
Chambersburg PA
CBHW030315270326
41926CB00010B/1379